THE EPISTLE TO THE GALATIANS

NEW TESTAMENT FOR SPIRITUAL READING

VOLUME 15

Edited by

John L. McKenzie, S.J.

THE EPISTLE
TO THE GALATIANS

GERHARD SCHNEIDER

CROSSROAD · NEW YORK

1981
The Crossroad Publishing Company
575 Lexington Avenue, New York, NY 10022

Originally published as *Der Brief an die Galater*
© 1964 by Patmos-Verlag
from the series *Geistliche Schriftlesung*
edited by Wolfgang Trilling
with Karl Hermann Schelke and Heinz Schürmann

English translation © 1969 by Burns & Oates, Limited, London
Translated by Kevin Smyth

Library of Congress Catalog Card Number: 81-68169
ISBN: 0-8245-0124-1

PREFACE

While the date of the Epistle to the Galatians is not entirely certain, there is no doubt that it is one of the earliest of Paul's epistles; and the problem which elicited its composition was the first major crisis in the apostolic church. The epistle is different from the other epistles in the way in which it plunges immediately after the greetings into the center of the question. The question is raised in abrupt, even harsh terms; and the reader will notice that the language of Paul is more severe concerning this question than it is towards some other questions which we might consider more important and urgent.

The primitive apostolic community was and considered itself to be a sect within Judaism. The earliest preachers addressed themselves to their fellow Jews and maintained the life of Jewish observances in which they had been reared. They proclaimed Jesus as the Messiah of Judaism, and presumably did not think that this proclamation could be addressed to others. The apostolate to the gentiles which Paul claims in this epistle (2:7-9) did not appear until some years after the formation of the primitive community; again the date is uncertain, but it had appeared before Paul became the chief apostle of the gentiles.

There is every indication that when the gospel was first proclaimed to the gentiles, it was proclaimed as an invitation to become Jewish Christians. The gentile converts undertook the obligation of the Jewish law at the same time that they received faith and baptism. It is doubtful that Paul was the first to conceive that faith in Christ did not imply the obligation of the law; but Paul was the first to present this teaching in its fullness, and to ground the teaching on the nature of Christian salvation itself. When Judaism was thus bypassed, the apostolic church faced its most serious crisis; for many, perhaps most, of the first Christians did not understand how a Christian could be anything but a Jew who believed in Jesus as Messiah.

The modern reader may find it difficult to grasp the importance of this question; or if he concedes that it was important to the primitive church, he may not see that the question has any meaning for him and his contemporaries. He knows that the problem was resolved before the end of the first century and that it has not arisen again since; and the Epistle to the Galatians may have for him no more than historical interest. But he should recall that the Epistle to the Galatians is a kind of sketch of the Epistle to the Romans, the longest, most doctrinal, and most quoted of the epistles of Paul. The implications of the Jewish-Christian question reach far and touch the most central articles of Christian belief.

Paul raises the question whether the saving act of God in Jesus Christ is sufficient. If the observance of the law is required, then something is lacking to the fullness of the saving act. It is a thesis of Paul that all men are enslaved by sin; if the Christians of the law were right, then they were partly saved already. Paul found this inconceivable. No one can add to the efficacy of the saving act or subtract from it. The totality of the saving act of Jesus Christ is a central article of Christian faith; no one affirmed it with such clarity before the Epistle to the Galatians.

Paul also raises the question of Christian unity. A division between Jewish Christians, presumably a higher grade, and gentile Christians, presumably a lower grade, would effectively create two churches. Because all men are equally saved by Jesus, other differences between men are reduced to insignificance. All have become sons of God, and in Christ there is neither Jew nor Greek, slave nor free, male nor female (3:28). Certainly this magnificent vision of Christian unity has not yet been realized in the church, nor has the church succeeded in making this vision genuinely attractive in the world to which it has a mission.

Paul also raises the question of Christian freedom. By New Testament times the law had become the most sacred institution of Judaism. By the law was meant the commandments of the five books of Moses, counted by the rabbis as 613, together with the " traditions of the elders " mentioned in the gospels. These traditions interpreted, applied, and expanded the biblical commandments so that they became a nearly complete code of conduct. By the observance of the law the Jew was assured of right relations with God; the law attempted as far as possible to cover every problem of conduct which could occur. Yet Paul, once a student of the rabbis, declared that the law was slavery from which Christ has delivered the Christian. No doubt there were some who thought of Christian freedom as an opportunity for the flesh (5:13); this dangerous misunderstanding was not a reason for limiting Christian freedom.

Christian freedom was for Paul in the first place liberation from the obligations of the law, the only obligations which Paul recognized as imposed by God. The moral system of Judaism was annulled, and Paul proposed no similar code to replace it. The whole law is now summed up in the single commandment to love one's neighbor as oneself (5:14). Paul believed that it was impossible to fulfill this commandment perfectly within the legal system of Judaism. To love perfectly one must be free of obligation. Love is the most personal decision one can make, and it must arise from an unfettered personal choice. How one is to love in practice must be left to the prudence of the individual person; and Paul seemed to think that the Christian should have little difficulty in distinguishing love from something else.

As we have mentioned, Paul took this problem very seriously. It is clear that he would not yield to the Judaizers even if it meant a division in the church. He was convinced that his gospel was the authentic gospel of Jesus, whatever might be the weight of those who preached a different gospel. He would not listen even if an angel had proclaimed the gospel of the Judaizers (1:8). Since the gospel as Paul proclaimed it has become the gospel of the church, we may pass over his assurance without remark. But how did Paul reach such assurance? One must suppose that no small amount of anguished thought and prayer was necessary before Paul took a firm position which may have been opposed by the majority of those whom he calls apostles.

The efficacy of the saving act of God in Jesus Christ, the unity of the church, and Christian freedom are not questions of purely antiquarian interest. It is important to us whether we believe that Jesus has effectively freed us from sin, and whether we fear that his deliverance was so incomplete and so ineffective that it needs to be supplemented by some other means. It is important to us whether the church is a single family of the children of God in which all are equal and no one is degraded or excluded. It is important to us whether our Christian unity is more important than the things which distinguish us from each other. It is important to us whether the church is a community of law or a community of love. The Epistle to the Galatians touches some of our most urgent contemporary problems, and it states the principles on which we can meet these problems.

The epistle illustrates the application of the gospel to a situa-

tion which was not implied in its original proclamation. Those
with whom Paul was engaged in controversy preached the true
gospel as far as they knew; and the church has always proclaimed the gospel with an incomplete awareness of its full
application. Orthodox preaching may have very limited horizons.
It may prefer that type of safety which is obtained by repeating
what has been said before. Clearly, Paul was a troublemaker in
the apostolic church. He upset an established order, even though
the order had not been long established. Were the principles of
Paul applied directly to some of our contemporary problems,
many would find them so radical as to be disturbing. Some
would prefer salvation through law rather than salvation through
love and a church not so perfectly unified that it would forbid
men to cherish their traditional divisions and enmities. The gospel of Paul is too simple for a complex world; but it was too
simple for the first century also. The epistle sums it up in a very
few statements which are quite easy to understand and quite
difficult to fulfill.

John L. McKenzie, S.J.

INTRODUCTION

The Gospel of Freedom

1. The Epistle to the Galatians was written by St. Paul to certain Christian communities who had been disturbed and even stirred to revolt by false brethren. The " Galatians " (3:1) were the Celtic inhabitants of the territory of Galatia in Asia Minor. They were the descendants of the Gauls who crossed the Danube and penetrated southwards into Asia Minor at the beginning of the third century B.C. Having settled down here, they later succeeded in setting up a kingdom which was transformed in 25 B.C. into the Roman province of Galatia.

a) Paul had twice visited the land of Galatia (Acts 16:6; 18:23). He evangelized the recipients of the Epistle to the Galatians on his second and third missionary journeys. On his second missionary journey, the Apostle visited first the communities which he had founded during his previous journey. Starting from Syria, he traveled as far as Pisidia, accompanied by Silas. He had brought Timothy along with him from Lystra. But the Holy Spirit " hindered " the three missionaries from following their original plan to travel on westwards into the province of Asia and its capital, Ephesus. They turned northwards and traveled through Phrygia " and the Galatian region " (Acts 16:6). It was probably an illness which detained the Apostle in the heart of Asia Minor; meanwhile (about A.D. 50), he preached the gospel to the Galatians (see Gal. 4:13). The missionaries then proceeded to Mysia, with the intention of reaching Bithynia. But once more, " the Spirit of Jesus would not allow them " to realize their plans (Acts 16:7). Unable to reach the districts along the Black Sea, they turned westwards and reached the coast of the Aegean at Troas. From there they crossed over to Europe for the first time (Acts 16:8-12). Some years after founding the Christian communities in Galatia, the Apostle visited them once more. It was at the beginning of his third missionary journey (about A.D. 55/56). According to the Acts of the Apostles, he traveled " first through the Galatian country and then through Phrygia, strengthening all the disciples " (Acts 18:23). Paul went on rather soon to Ephesus, where he stayed for two or three years (Acts 19:10; 20:31).

b) Bad news came from the Christian communities in Galatia while Paul was working in Ephesus. This would have been about A.D. 56. The gospel is threatened among the Galatians. Strange missionaries have penetrated the community. They take the standpoint of an extreme Jewish Christianity. They demand circumcision of the Galatian Christians (Gal. 5:2f., 6, 12; 6:12f.), who had come to Christianity from paganism. They throw the young churches into confusion by declaring that men cannot be saved without the circumcision demanded by the Jewish law. Their success in sowing confusion evidently inspires them to become real agitators. The flock is attacked by " savage wolves " (see Acts 20:29). Paul grasps the situation at once. What is at stake is whether men are to be saved by the law or by the grace of Jesus Christ. The summons to submit to circumcision is ultimately dictated by the belief that men are to be saved by fulfilling the precepts of the law. The false teachers also insist on the observation of certain days in a religious calendar (Gal. 4:1-10). The keeping of fixed dates does not mean merely adopting a religion based on law: it also means a relapse into the worship of pagan gods (4:8-10). Along with the slogans of circumcision and the calendar, the intruders are distinguished by something which at first sight seems to contradict the agitators' fanatical devotion to the law. The false teachers clearly do not keep the whole law themselves (see 5:3; 6:13). A strong urge for self-assertion and an illusory pride in their own powers (5:13, 26; 6:3f., 7) lead the Galatians themselves to look on themselves as "spiritual" (6:1) and above the "unspiritual" and "elementary" affairs of morality. The provisional success of the new teachers among the Galatians is only possible because these Jewish-Christian zealots can undermine Paul's authority. They bring the Apostle and his activity into contempt. He ingratiates himself, they maintain, by currying favor. Above all, he does not derive his message from revelation, as do Peter and the other apostles (see chs. 1-2). This argument of the innovators only makes sense if they themselves claim to be supported by the apostles, which is false. Thus the Galatian communities are going through a crisis with regard to the authority which they are to follow. This leads to a crisis with regard to the faith which they are to believe. This crisis of faith then endangers the salvation of the Galatians.

2. How does Paul, who is the father of these gentile Christian churches, intervene in this dangerous situation? He writes a letter which is meant to offset the danger. Paul writes in full consciousness of his apostolic responsibility; his tone is sharp and passionate. The letter is not a treatise of theology. No systematic structure can be discerned in it. But it has a very clear and definite theme: Paul counters the crisis of confidence by pointing to the divine origin of his apostolic office. He straightens out the crisis of faith by asking for a decision between law and

freedom, works of the law and the obedience of faith. He concludes by showing how a life of loving service should grow out of faith.

a) Paul deliberately begins his letter with a description of his call to the apostolic office (1 : 13-24). He does not enter upon a discussion and leave his imperilled flock to judge the intrinsic value of his arguments. He starts with the assertion that his vocation as an apostle and his preaching as an apostle, the gospel, come from God himself. He is " an apostle, not from men, and not through a man, but through Jesus Christ and God the Father " (1 : 1). What the Apostle preaches is not human wisdom but God's word to man (1 : 11f.). Hence men are not asked to pass judgment upon it, because it stands or falls with the charge of him who preaches it. Paul has his gospel from Christ. And therefore he has authority. There is only one gospel (1 : 6f.). Even if " an angel from heaven " were to preach another gospel than the Pauline one, " let him be accursed " (1 : 8). Paul is conscious that his charge was given him by God, so he can speak clearly and with assurance, without having to plead for understanding. Still, he tries to make it easy for the Galatians to come to a reasoned grasp of the faith. They are to acknowledge that Paul received his message by divine revelation. The change in the Pharisee Paul which turned him from a zealot for the law into a preacher of the good news of the grace of God did not come from instruction and from a gradual growth in understanding (1 : 12). It came from God (1 : 15f.). Though Paul had only meager relations with the apostles in Jerusalem after his call (1 : 17-24), his message was in accord with that of the primitive community, and they recognized its truth (2 : 1-10). Finally, Paul emphasizes that he had upheld the truth of the gospel at Antioch in face of Peter (2 : 11-14). What is the " truth of the gospel "

(2:5.14) which Paul had already defended once and which must now be defended again before the Galatians?

b) The truth of the gospel is that we attain salvation by faith and not through the works of the law. It was from the preaching of faith and not from the works of the law that the Galatians received the Holy Spirit (3:2). The gift of the Spirit is the beginning of salvation (Rom. 8:23). Man is one day to have the fullness of salvation in this Spirit (Rom. 8:15-30). But the Christians of Galatia are doing their best " to end in the flesh " (Gal. 3:3). They look on the law of the old covenant not just as a precept but—loyal to the preaching of the Jewish agitators—as the way to salvation. That is why they are ready to be circumcised. For Paul, this is a blow at the very heart of the gospel message of salvation. It is not a matter of asking whether the baptized Christian should " still also " obey the directives of the law. This is the decisive question: Do we gain salvation by the grace of the crucified Christ Jesus (3:1), or do we acquire justice before God by accomplishing the law? Paul puts the emphasis on grace in a radical way! For " if righteousness were through the law, then Christ died for nothing " (2:21). Faith, and not accomplishments which lead to self-righteousness, sets up the right relationship between man and God. This is also the message of Jesus (see Mk. 1:15; Lk. 17:10; 18:9-14). Paul understood this message and took up its defense. It was this that prevented the church of Jesus from becoming a Jewish sect. That does not mean that the Pharisaic type of piety, which is centered on personal achievement, has been conquered forever in the church. The spirit of faith is not that of a servile performance of obedience but the joyous spirit of childlike submissiveness in freedom and love. The law was our tutor—until Christ came. But now we are no longer in the charge of this tutor (3:19-25). We are free, the children

who inherit the blessing which was promised to Abraham (3 : 6-9).
" Neither circumcision nor uncircumcision counts, but a new
creation " (6 : 15). This is the principle which has been in force
since the death of Christ (6 : 14-16).

c) Though Paul announces the gospel of freedom to the
Galatians, he is well aware that freedom can be abused as a pre-
text for sin. Freedom can easily be confused with libertinism.
" You were called to freedom, brethren; only do not let freedom
become an incitement for the flesh, but be servants of one
another through love " (5 : 13). It cannot be said with certainty
whether the false teachers preached libertinism in Galatia or—
as is more likely—Paul warned his readers against it because the
false teachers had misrepresented his preaching as allowing unbridled liberty. Freedom therefore does not mean license. Freedom means love. But love is not to be just a notion. And so Paul
urges the Galatians to love their neighbor, where self-deception is
less likely than in the love of God. " The whole law is fulfilled in
one word, ' You shall love your neighbor as yourself ' " (5 : 14).
Here the Apostle is once more following the message of Jesus
(Mk. 12 : 28-31). Freedom does not mean being rid of all obligations. It is rather a freedom that strives to take the initiative, eager
and inventive in serving others in love. This true love stems from
faith (5 : 6); it is produced by faith, because genuine faith becomes
effective in love. This love is also the " fruit of the Spirit " (5 : 22).
The Holy Spirit is the author of this Christian way of life. He
is also the field in which man must sow if he is one day to harvest
eternal life (6 : 8).

OUTLINE

xvii

THE OPENING OF THE LETTER
(1:1-5)

Signature and Address (1:1-2)

1Paul, an apostle not from men, and not through a man, but through Jesus Christ and God the Father, who raised him from the dead . . .

The name of the sender comes at the beginning of the letter. But Paul adds at once the title of Apostle to the name. Thus he gives his letter an official character from the start. To be an apostle is to be an " envoy " equipped with a message and authority. He has been charged with a duty to perform. The Jewish diaspora was acquainted with such authorized envoys as early as pre-Christian times. They came in the name of the central authorities at Jerusalem to visit the communities of the diaspora. The Christian notion of apostle has the same meaning. Only here the charge is given by Christ.

Paul stresses the fact that his mission does not derive from men. And he has not received his authority through a man. Clearly, that is what has been forgotten in the communities of Galatia. The false teachers who have penetrated into the communities since the Apostle founded them and visited them are contesting Paul's apostolic authority. They have probably belittled the Apostle by saying that he does not belong to the Twelve whom Jesus chose and charged with their mission. Paul, they say, was not with Jesus from the beginning, and hence cannot be an apostle. Once this argument evoked a response, suspicion could be cast on the preaching of Paul.

The question must be taken very seriously. To be an apostle is it necessary to have known Jesus during his life on earth? In the supplementary choice of the apostle Matthias, this was the decisive qualification demanded (Acts 1:21f.). But Jesus Christ had chosen still another instrument for his work and had made him an apostle, though not by this " normal " way. No one can fix his ways for him; he is free in his decisions and acts.

Paul is an envoy through Jesus Christ. His apostolic charge was given him by Christ. He received it on the way to Damascus. He is well aware of the fact that Peter and the rest of the Twelve had seen the risen Lord earlier (1 Cor. 15:5), and that he himself is " the least of the apostles, not worthy to be called an apostle " because he had persecuted the church of God. But he also knows that he is an apostle through God's grace (1 Cor. 15:8-10). It is, therefore, with the message and the authority of Christ that Paul addressed the Galatians and addresses them again now. It is Christ himself who also confronts us through Paul.

Behind Jesus Christ stands God the Father. By naming him after Christ here, Paul undoubtedly means to designate the Father as the ultimate source of the apostolic office. The apostolic authority comes ultimately from the divine mandate, not from the mandate of human authority. In the revelation of Christ on the way to Damascus, Paul experienced God as him who raised Jesus from the dead. He is the living God, the creator who is still working today—in the resurrection of the Son, but also in the vocation of Paul. The creative power of God is a present reality.

2. . . and all the brethren who are with me, to the churches of Galatia.

The letter is sent by other Christians as well as Paul. They are co-signatories. Their names are not mentioned. But Paul attaches importance to the fact that he is in accord with the brethren when he writes and teaches. He is not thinking so much of individuals as of the general body of the brethren. The Apostle speaks not merely by virtue of his apostolic authority but also in accord with all his fellow Christians. The faith of the church is a norm for the various communities. An individual can err, but the whole church enjoys the assistance of the Lord and his Spirit.

The recipients of the letter are the churches of Galatia. It is intended for several Christian communities in the region of Galatia. The letter is a circular letter which is to be passed on from community to community. All the communities are menaced by the same danger of being lured out of the fellowship of the faith by the false teachers. They should think of the greater fellowship to which they belong.

Paul addresses the Christians very briefly as " the churches of Galatia " though he knows them well. Having begun by referring to his apostolic office, he omits something which he includes in nearly all his later letters to churches. He assigns no title of honor to the " churches of Galatia." He does not call the Galatians the " church of God " (2 Cor. 1:1), " those sanctified in Christ Jesus " (1 Cor. 1:2), " beloved of God, elect and holy " (Rom. 1:7), " saints in Christ Jesus " (Phil. 1:1). " Mark how he already shows his deep displeasure here," says St. John Chrysostom in his ancient commentary. The reserve with which Paul expresses himself is certainly not merely to teach his readers a lesson. It also manifests his very human feelings of displeasure. Only once does he address the Galatians as " my children " (4:19). Elsewhere, the predominant form of address is the brief " brethren." The Apostle's " displeasure " does not distort his view. He knows that he is still talking to men who are his brothers.

Greeting (1:3-5)

³*Grace to you and peace from God our Father and the Lord Jesus Christ . . .*

The greeting which Paul now sends to his readers both prays for and conveys a blessing. Grace and peace are not merely prayed for; they really come down " upon " the Galatians (see 6:16). The Apostle's greeting is therefore more than good wishes. When he greets the community, he really imparts the blessing of heaven.

Grace is primarily to be understood as the good will, the gracious attitude which marks God's actions. It governs his action even towards the sinful and mistaken. Paul assigns the Galatians, who are going to be the object of bitter reproaches on his part, to this region of divine grace. While Jewish theology was convinced that all the " mercy " of God had to do in the last resort was to make up for the margin which human effort had left unfulfilled, the Christian knows that he is, from first to last, dependent on the " grace " of God.

Peace comes from God. For Christians as for the Jews before them, the word meant more than untroubled relationships between man and his God. Peace is simply salvation, the sum total of all that God wills to bestow upon man and all that man desires to have from God.

Grace and peace are given by God the Father. They are conveyed by Jesus Christ, who is our Lord. Grace is, as it were, the atmosphere which God has created through Christ, and in which peace comes to be. It is the atmosphere which Paul conveys by his greeting. And he also makes the result, the peace of God, effective among the Galatians.

... who sacrificed himself for our sins, to rescue us from the present world of wickedness according to the will of God and our Father.

Paul cannot speak of the heavenly Lord and future judge, Jesus Christ, without mentioning at once the act of Jesus the Messiah from which God's salvation flows. The object of God's salvific action in Christ was the deliverance of men.

Christ has delivered himself to death. His death is essentially self-dedication, obedience. Just as the Old Testament speaks of the servant of the Lord and his giving himself as an expiation, so Paul says that Jesus " sacrificed himself " freely. Christ died for the sins of men. That means that he went to his death because we have sinned and in order to redeem us from sin.

But Paul stresses the object of the death of the Lord. He is not thinking here of a result that has already taken place; he speaks of an intention of Christ which is still being envisaged, in accordance with the will of the heavenly Father. Christ wishes to rescue us from the present world of wickedness. The wicked world which strives against us is a menacing power from which we are to be rescued. Paul is not asserting it as a general statement; he is thinking of the Galatians. What is happening to them reveals the menace of the power at work in this world and age. It shows itself in the fact that the communities are being ensnared by legalism. According to the will of God, who is our kindly Father, man should be free from such entanglements. And the Christian already belongs to the new age of freedom. He is far ahead of his times. A religion of law, which looks for salvation from the fulfillment of precepts, would be a relapse into the old but present world in which Israel lives. The death of Jesus Christ has brought on a new world, the new creation (6:15) of which the prophets

of the ancient covenant spoke. These are wide horizons which
the Apostle opens up here. The particular interests which Paul
goes on to discuss must be viewed against this vast background.
The Christian can only judge and answer life's questions in the
light of the death of Christ.

⁵*To whom be glory for ever and ever. Amen.*

The heading of the letter closes with praise of God, who is the
author of our salvation, the Father whose will Christ followed as
he freed us. Such doxologies were common in Judaism. They
were added almost conventionally to every mention of God. But
in Paul's writings, the custom is not merely traditional, it is
meaningful in the extreme. When he has occasion to speak of one
of the wonderful works of God, he puts in one of these doxologies. The practice was rooted in the liturgy, as it also seems to
have been among the Jews. When the salvific works of God are
proclaimed in divine worship, the community responds by prais-
ing his name. So Paul too gives glory to God for Christ's work
of salvation. Wherever the Christian perceives the works of
God's salvation, he feels the urge to give thanks.

The final " Amen," which confirms what was said in the intro-
duction, is likewise an echo of the liturgy. In the Epistle to the
Galatians it lends particular weight to what has gone before.
" That is how things are and should be." We are to recognize
that God has granted us salvation and that glory is due to him.
It is not man who brings about his own salvation. God is the
redeemer. He has brought on the new creation.

THE BODY OF THE LETTER
(1:6—6:10)

PAUL RECEIVED HIS GOSPEL BY REVELA-
TION, AND HIS APOSTOLIC MISSION
FROM GOD AND CHRIST (1:6—2:21)

The Epistle to the Galatians is a piece of polemical writing. Accord-
ingly, it lacks systematic structure. Nonetheless, it may be divided
into three parts. The first part of the text is clearly marked off from
the two following parts. Paul defends his apostolic office against the
accusations of the false teachers in Galatia after having mentioned the
occasion of his letter: the truth of the gospel as Paul had preached it
is endangered among the Christians of Galatia (1:6-10). Hence the
Apostle must demonstrate that he has received this gospel directly
from Christ himself. The assertion (1:11f.) is followed by three proofs.
Paul did not learn the gospel from his studies but from Christ, who
made the zealous Pharisee an apostle (1:13-24). Thus this gospel is not
the work of man. Still, it is none other than that of the first apostles,
for these have recognized the gospel of Paul (2:1-10). Hence Paul
could finally uphold the truth of the gospel even when faced with
Peter, whose false attitude at Antioch was dictated by timidity
(2:11-21). This episode, which had already served to demonstrate the
truth of the Pauline gospel, leads Paul to the second part of his pole-
mic, which is already suggested in 2:15-21. The third part deals with
the content of the gospel from which the Galatians are tempted to
apostatize.

The Occasion of the Letter: The Truth of the Gospel is at Stake among the Galatians (1:6-10)

Having saluted his readers with a blessing, the Apostle hastens at
once to take up his theme. The greeting is not followed by a word of

thanks to God, as in his other letters. Without further ado, he turns to the occasion of the letter. He does not thank God for what he has done in the churches of Galatia; or rather, he omits to voice his thanksgiving. The work of God among the Galatians is in danger, their faith is wavering.

Disturbance Caused by False Teachers (1:6-7)

⁶I am amazed that you are falling away so quickly from him who has called you unto grace, and turning to another gospel, ⁷which does not exist; but there are certain people who are disturbing you and trying to distort the gospel of Christ.

The Apostle finds himself amazed at the turn of events in Galatia, where defections have occurred so rapidly. It is probably less than a year since Paul visited the communities, and the new converts are already allowing themselves to be turned away from God, who had called them into the realm of grace. When Greek-speaking Christians pronounced the word " community," " church," their " *ekklesia* " evoked the thought of their being called by God into the fellowship of his people. There they were sure of the favor and the special fatherly goodness of God. They were his beloved children.

The Apostle can only be amazed, therefore, to find the Christians of Galatia ready to turn away from God and turn to something which does not exist. No other gospel exists except that which Paul has proclaimed. For one thing, it is—like the gospel preached by the other apostles—the one gospel of Jesus Christ. For another, what the innovators are preaching in Galatia is contrary to the very nature of the gospel, which is to be good news. The gospel of Jesus is the good news about God's fatherly

kindness and the liberation of men. But the new teachers want
to lay the yoke of the law once more on the neck of Christians,
while Jesus' message is " Come to me, all who labor and are
heavy-laden, and I will refresh you. Take my yoke upon you,
and learn from me, for I am gentle and humble-hearted, and you
will find refreshment for your souls. For my yoke is soft and
my burden is light " (Mt. 11 : 28-30).

Hence to turn from him who has called men to grace is to
clutch at the void, to be ensnared by illusions. Someone thinks he
is hearing a new gospel. But the new doctrine which he hears can
only be false, and impose a heavy yoke.

The false teachers, of course, can only be successful because
they give out their doctrine as the gospel. This causes disturbance
and confusion. They appeal to Jesus and his apostles, but
wrongly. How can Christians distinguish the true message of the
Lord from false teaching? Certainly, it is not always easy. However, one thing is characteristic and indispensable in the true
message of Jesus: it is glad news and not a heavy yoke.

The gospel of Christ does not consist merely of what Christ
proclaimed. He himself is the essential content of what he and
his apostles preached. The resurrection of Christ from the dead
means the beginning of a new creation. That too is good news.
Finally, the gospel of Christ means also that Christ himself
comes to meet us in the proclamation of the gospel. The
Christian is not dealing with a law and its inculcation when he
hears the gospel. He is meeting the living Lord, Christ.

The Pauline Gospel Must not be Perverted (1:8-9)

⁸But even if we ourselves or an angel from heaven were to

*preach a gospel instead of that which we have preached to you,
let him be accursed.*

If Christ presents himself in the preaching of the gospel, any
distortion of the message is an attack on Christ himself. That
is why Paul can anathematize anyone who tries to falsify the
gospel. It is no light matter. Even if he himself, the Apostle, or
even if a heavenly messenger tried to change the gospel, a curse
should come upon them. Paul utters this curse by virtue of his
authority and his mission. The effect of the wish and the
formula, which derive from the Old Testament, is to exclude
the offender from the community of Christ. It is still only a
threat here, uttered to bring home the seriousness and the importance of such a perversion of God's message and to deter possible
offenders. In certain cases this " curse," exclusion from the
community, was imposed in New Testament times, as in the
case of the man at Corinth who was guilty of incest. There,
however, we are also told that the expulsion of the sinner was
meant to help him to amend and be converted. It did not mean
final exclusion from eternal salvation (1 Cor. 5 : 1-5). The church
acts as successor to the apostles when it watches over the truth
and purity of the gospel. But in doing so, it must be as deeply
serious as the Apostle, because God is in question and not earthly
interests. Hence excommunication, which means exclusion from
the community and in particular from the Eucharist, still exists
today, as the severest measure of church discipline. But all the
ways of love and brotherly care must first have been tried (see
Mt. 18 : 15-17).

⁹*As we have said before, so now I repeat: if anyone preaches a
gospel instead of that which you have received, let him be
accursed.*

The Apostle pronounces the anathema once more. Having just
envisaged the most extreme case, that of himself or even an
angel distorting the gospel, he now points to those who are
actually perverting the message of Christ in Galatia. Paul de-
livers these unnamed opponents of Christ to judgment. He is
undoubtedly deeply angered. But his anger is not caused by a
jealous egoism. It comes from his anxiety about the purity of
the gospel. Anger can be justified if it springs from the love of
Christ and loyalty to the gospel.

The Apostle is in the Service of God and Christ (1:10)

10a*Am I now seeking the favor of men, or of God? Or am I
trying to please men?*

The false teachers must have tried to belittle Paul in the eyes of
the Galatians by reproaching him with trying to please men
when he spoke of the freedom of the Christian. This was his way
of beguiling them and winning their support. Paul now counters
them by asking whether the sharp curses which he has just
pronounced sound like " wheedling " (1:8f.). They are anything
but flattery. The obvious conclusion is that the Apostle speaks
in these terms in order to please God. For when he curses those
who distort the message of his Son, his intention is to obey the
will of God. No, Paul does not tell people what they want to
hear. His one desire is to be able to face God.

10b*If I were still trying to please men, I should not be a slave of
Christ.*

The bitter questions are followed by an almost mournful reflection. Paul had once tried to please men. It was when he was persecuting the church in his Pharisaic zeal. But since he has seen Christ, his heavenly Lord, he has become his slave. This is the right view of the apostolic charge. The envoy of Christ must be a servant. "This is how one should regard us, as servants of Christ and stewards of the mysteries of God. Moreover, it is required of stewards that they should be found trustworthy" (1 Cor. 4:1f.). Paul speaks as an Apostle here, one who knows that he is a slave (*doulos*). The Greek word implies all the dependence of the slave, the loyalty of the servant, the submissiveness and also the nobility of one, who, like the Old Testament prophets, can be the "servant of the Lord."

The Truth of the Pauline Gospel rests on the Divine Revelation given to the Apostle (1:11—2:21)

The Apostle's Testimony: The Gospel Comes from Christ 1:11-12)

[11]*For I would have you know, brethren, that the gospel which was preached by me is no mere human thing.* [12]*For I did not receive it from any man, nor was I taught it, but it came through a revelation of Jesus Christ.*

Solemnly and forcibly, Paul puts forward his fundamental assertion. He addresses the Galatians as brothers, as though he were trying to gain a sympathetic hearing. The Apostle appeals to the fellowship which already exists and which demands that each should be ready to listen to the other, when fundamental matters are in question. A brother should not turn a deaf ear to a brother.

What is at stake is the essence of the Pauline gospel. What Paul has preached among the Galatians is not a human invention. It is not a wisdom thought out by men for which one pleads and argues. It is not a matter of gaining insight into an important truth, and of being glad to be able to lead others to the same understanding.

Paul, just as the first apostles, received his gospel from Christ. The origin of the message is to be found in Christ. That is the important thing for Paul now. He is not arguing from the intrinsic merits of his message. After all, it does not consist primarily of a doctrine whose correctness can be examined and weighed; first and foremost, the gospel proclaims historical events. Hence Paul points to the source of his message. He received it by direct revelation from Jesus.

This revelation is an unveiling of divine mysteries which are not accessible to natural experience. If God did not draw back the veil, these supernatural facts would not be available to men. The revelation in which God made his Son visible to Paul empowered and charged Paul to proclaim Christ as the risen Lord. Because Jesus did not perish in death, because he was raised from the dead, he is the heavenly Lord. That is the gospel which Paul received by a revelation of Jesus Christ. When the gospel thus revealed is brought to men, men cannot encounter it with questioning, research, and investigations but only with thankful acceptance in faith.

Paul did not learn his gospel by being instructed. It was not by being taught as a pupil is by an instructor, a disciple by a master, that Paul came by his gospel. Instruction is given by men to men, revelation comes from on high. We have to note, however, that at this point the Apostle is obliged to stress the fact that his message in its origin is independent of the tradition of the other apostles. That does not mean that it is different from the gospel preached by the others. On the contrary, Paul also has definite traditions to hand on which he himself received from tradition. The fact that the message of the gospel is a revelation, that it comes from Christ, helps us to solve clearly and certainly human problems which remain enigmas to ordinary thinking.

Proof from Paul's Behavior before and after his Call (1:13-24)

There remains the question of the reality of the manifestation in which, as Paul affirms, Jesus Christ was revealed to him. Paul now justifies his solemn declaration.

PAUL WAS A FANATICAL PHARISEE (1:13–14)

¹³For you have heard of my former conduct in Judaism, how I persecuted the church of God violently and tried to destroy it . . .

The Galatians are already acquainted with the Apostle's past. He must have told them of it himself. He had not sought to hide it. He calls attention to it now because his Jewish past is a proof that he could not have received the gospel from those whom he persecuted fanatically.

Paul was deeply rooted in the Jewish religion. That is the reason why he persecuted the church. In the eyes of a Jew like Paul it was a community of apostates. He persecuted it savagely, bent on its destruction. Now he knows that this fellowship is the " church of God." It is God's chosen people. And hence his hostility was directed against God himself.

¹⁴. . . and how I made progress in Judaism more than many of

*my contemporaries among the people, being extraordinarily zeal-
ous for the traditions of my fathers.*

The persecutor made progress in Judaism. In persecuting the
church, he was not playing false in any way to his Jewish way of
life. He was rather steeping himself more thoroughly in that
mentality. Compared to his contemporaries, who acted perhaps
from a sense of duty, Paul was a persecutor because of his deepest
convictions.

Paul was zealously devoted to the traditions of his forefathers.
He was a true Pharisee, and therefore the traditions of the fathers
were as valid in his eyes as the law of Moses. These traditions,
which originated in an effort to interpret the law given on Mount
Sinai and to apply it to changing conditions of life, were observed
as literally by a genuine Pharisee as the law itself. They formed
the " hedge," by which the law was to be protected. It was in
view of these traditions that Jesus spoke out against Pharisaic
Judaism (see Mk. 7:1-13). The Pharisee went so far as to trans-
gress the law of God for the sake of these traditions! Since Paul
was a Pharisee, he had had a profound experience of this way of
life and piety. He was to denounce this " legalism " as false and
misleading.

But Paul is not a renegade who consigns to the flames what he
has once adored. Even as a Christian he speaks with reverence
of " his " people, of the traditions of " his " fathers. The wish of
his heart and his prayer to God are for " their salvation " (Rom.
10:1). " For I bear witness for them, that they have zeal for God,
but without understanding; for since they did not know the
righteousness of God, and sought to set up their own, they
failed to submit themselves to the righteousness of God " (Rom.
10:2-3).

THE GOSPEL CAME FROM GOD (1:15-17)

15But when he who had set me apart since I was in my mother's womb, and had called me by his grace, was pleased 16ato reveal his Son to me . . .

God was pleased to reveal his Son to the persecutor of the church. The manifestation of the Son of God to Paul comes by the free decision of God's will. God puts into execution what he has decreed in his good pleasure. No one would have thought it possible that the persecutor of the church could become an apostle. But God executed his plan outside Damascus.

God had already set Paul apart, like a prophet, while he was still in his mother's womb. This singling out means that God sequestrates a man, consecrates and sanctifies him for his service. Here the service was to be the proclamation of the gospel. The Apostle is an instrument in the hand of God.

The call of Paul is a work of divine grace. Paul did not become an apostle of Christ through profound meditation or honest good will. It is not a matter of a " conversion " brought about by better knowledge or upright effort. Paul was called to be an apostle by the irruption of God's grace.

16b. . . in order that I should preach him among the gentiles . . .

Just as Jeremiah became in his vocation " a prophet for the (pagan) peoples " (Jer. 1:5), so too the messianic prophet of the Lord was not merely " to restore the tribes of Jacob and bring back the remnants of Israel " (Is. 49:6a), but rather, his message was to be world-wide. " I will make you the light of the nations, so that my salvation shall reach to the ends of the earth " (Is.

49:6b). The child whom Simeon was privileged to take into his arms was to be " a light for the revelation of the gentiles " (Lk. 2:32). The mission of Paul, the Apostle of the gentiles, was to be equally universal. "This man is my chosen instrument, to carry my name before nations and kings and the children of Israel " (Acts 9:15).

Christ himself is named here as the main content of the gospel. He is to be proclaimed as the good news. In the gospel Christ himself speaks. But Christ is the risen, heavenly Lord, who has come for the whole world and turns to all men, not only to Israel.

[16c]. . . *then at once, without taking counsel of flesh and blood,* [17]*and without going up to Jerusalem to the apostles who were called before me, I went away to Arabia, and then returned once more to Damascus.*

The call to the apostolate was linked with the charge of preaching to the whole world. From where did Paul derive the contents of his preaching? He did not take it over and learn it from flesh and blood, that is, from man. He received it with his call. That was enough for his preaching. Paul did not need to discuss his revelation. He took his decision at once. Hence he cannot have received his gospel from other men. It came to him from God and not from any man. The heart of the gospel cannot be " found " by human thinking. When Peter confessed that Jesus was the Messiah, Jesus answered: " Flesh and blood have not revealed it to you, but my Father in heaven " (Mt. 16:17).

Paul did not seek consultations with other Christians after his conversion. Indeed, he did not even take the way to Jerusalem. So his gospel remained unaffected, just as he had received it. It was not disregard for the first apostles that led him to act thus, but his consciousness of being fully their equal. Paul too is an apostle. It was only much later, by divine direction, that he presented his gospel before the apostles in Jerusalem for their judgment (2:1f.).

He made no contacts with the primitive community. On the contrary, he went first to Arabia. This means the region south-west of Damascus, the northern portion of the kingdom of the Nabateans, which was non-Jewish territory. In all probability, the Apostle had already begun his missionary work there. In any case, the Arabia in question was not a desert into which Paul withdrew. It was an inhabited region. From there he returned again to Damascus. Thus the origin of the Pauline gospel remained uninfluenced by any human being.

FEW RELATIONS WITH THE FIRST APOSTLES (1:18–20)

18Then, three years later, I went up to Jerusalem, to visit Cephas, and I stayed with him for a fortnight.

It was not only in the first years after his call that the relations between Paul and the other apostles were sparse. They remained so for more than ten years. When he visited Jerusalem for the first time after his Damascus experience, two full years had passed. And he did not go with any intention of submitting his gospel to the inspection of the primitive community. He went in order to make the acquaintance of the man to whom the Lord had given the name of " the Rock " (*kepha*). Paul is anxious not to present his visit to the head of the apostles as anything very important. He emphasizes the fact that he stayed with Peter for only a fortnight. Three years are contrasted with two weeks. In the brief space of two weeks the gospel of Paul cannot have been radically affected.

The motive of his journey to Jerusalem is given clearly in the term which Paul uses to describe his visit to Peter. He wishes to get to know Peter because Peter occupies a preëminent place. St. John Chrysostom, with his fine feeling for the Greek language, says that Paul uses the term " visit " in the same sense as " when people say that they wish to see great and famous cities." Since the apostles have the same charge as he, Paul wants to know them personally.

[19]*I saw no other apostle, only James, the brother of the Lord.*

Peter was the only member of the group of the apostles whom Paul then met in Jerusalem. Apart from Peter, Paul met only James, one of the so-called " brothers of the Lord." At the beginning he had as little comprehension of Jesus' work as his other relatives, but he was singled out by the risen Lord and granted an apparition (1 Cor. 15 : 7). In the primitive community he was to hold a leading place. Obviously, Paul paid him only a very brief visit. His object in coming to Jerusalem was to meet Peter.

[20]*Before God, what I am writing to you is no lie.*

From the Galatians' point of view, some twenty years after the visit to Jerusalem, it may seem strange that Paul met no other apostles. Just as we so easily do today, most people regarded the primitive community of Jerusalem as one of the headquarters of the preachers of the faith, a sort of central mission where one could always find the Twelve. Paul assures his readers with an oath that things happened as he described them. He asserts it before God's face. God is his witness.

PAUL REMAINED PERSONALLY UNKNOWN TO THE COMMUNITIES OF JUDEA (1:21–24)

²¹*Then I came to the countries of Syria and Cilicia.* ²²*But I was personally unknown to the Christian churches of Judea.*

After the visit to Jerusalem, Paul took up work in his own missionary field. He traveled northwards and preached in Syria, where the first city communities of gentile Christians were to be found, in its capital, Antioch. Then he went on further north to Cilicia, where his native city Tarsus was situated. Here too, any Jerusalem influence on the preaching of his gospel can be excluded. Paul is now working once more in pagan lands. The Christian communities of Judea, the country around Jerusalem, do not know him by sight. They have heard about him. But Paul did not stay with them, much less work among them as an apostle.

These Jewish-Christian churches are called "churches in Christ." There was still no term in existence for "Christian." The difference between a Jewish and a Christian community in a given place is that the latter live "in Christ," that is, in the realm where their Lord works and rules.

²³*They had only heard that he who had once persecuted us, now preaches the faith which he tried to destroy,* ²⁴ *and they praised God for me.*

The Jewish communities know Paul only by reputation. They surely cannot have influenced the preaching of the Apostle. They learn with astonishment and thanksgiving that the persecutor of yesterday is preaching the faith today. If he had once played havoc with the faith, he is now building it up. Faith here means more than the individual act of faith. It is what divides Christian from Jew, for whom the law is the way of salvation. It is the power of the message of faith, the new reality of God among us.

It is not only astonishment that greets the news of the change in the persecutor, who has become a preacher of the faith. The communities respond with thanksgiving and praise to God. They know that this is not just a strange turn in human destiny but that the grace of God has acted efficaciously on Paul. The church responds by blessing and thanking God.

They think of Paul in this praise of God. His call is a blessing for the whole church, which suffers from each one's sins and benefits by each one's grace as God exalts him. When God revealed his Son to him, Paul received his apostolic office. With this, the proof has been given that he did not receive his gospel from man. That is excluded both by what preceded and followed the manifestation of Christ to him.

Further Proof: The First Apostles Recognized Paul's Preaching and his Apostolic Office (2 :1–10)

PAUL PUT HIS GOSPEL BEFORE THE APOSTLES IN JERUSALEM (2 :1–5)

¹Then, fourteen years later, I went up once more to Jerusalem, along with Barnabas, taking Titus with me.

Fourteen years passed before Paul went back to Jerusalem. It was a long time. During these years, Paul, true to his missionary vocation, had been active among the gentile converts who were his special object of interest. He stresses at the beginning of the sentence the long passage of years in order to show that his preaching remained independent. The missionary finds the courage for the long haul in the certainty he has of his vocation.

His companion on the trip to Jerusalem was Barnabas, the son of Jewish parents living abroad in Cyprus. His real name was Joseph, and the designation " Barnabas " means " son of prophecy." He was probably one of the inspired Christian prophets. The Galatians must have known him by repute as an important figure. He had arrived at Jerusalem in the early days, and had been sent to the great international city of Antioch as the trusted delegate of the Jerusalem community. He was responsible too for bringing Paul to Antioch, and he accompanied him on his first missionary journey. Thus Barnabas and Paul both had the same background. They were born and bred among the Jewish diaspora, and hence were particularly well suited for the gentile mission.

Paul took a helper along with him, Titus. Titus was a " Greek " (2:3), that is, of a pagan family. Though Titus had not been circumcised (2:3), Paul took him with him. Perhaps this was the very reason why he brought him to Jerusalem—in view of the prospective debate about the validity of the law. Personal contacts can help to bridge differences of opinion more easily.

[2]I went in consequence of a revelation. And I put before them the gospel which I preach among the gentiles, in a special meeting with the men of repute, to make sure I was not running, or had not run in vain.

The journey was not undertaken on Paul's own initiative, and it was not suggested by a sense of personal uncertainty. It was the consequence of a revelation given by God. Precisely how this revelation came does not matter. The important thing is that the Apostle allows himself to be guided from on high. The Acts of the Apostles also shows how Paul follows the guidance of the Holy Spirit in his work. It is God himself who propels the mission onward and leads it to its goal.

The object of his journey was to present his gospel to the Jerusalem community in the form in which he had been preaching it for fifteen years. A divine directive had impelled him to have his gospel ratified by the primitive community. The Apostle is absolutely convinced that there is only one gospel, that which he has been preaching. But he is equally sure that there are apostles in Jerusalem. At God's command he went to talk things over with them. That the discussion ended with a decision in favor of Paul is already indicated in the way he writes to the Galatians: he is still preaching today the same gospel which he had always preached among the gentiles.

The decision can only be given by the " men of repute." He means the apostles, who are the authorities in the community. God refers him to them, not them to him. They were apostles before him. It is a principle revealed by God that in questions of unity one must look to the origins.

Paul is impelled by a real anxiety. Not that he was unsure of himself. He compares his activity with the unremitting effort of a runner in a race. " Do you not know that all the competitors run in the games, but that only one receives the prize?" (1 Cor. 9:24). And he writes to the Christians of Philippi: " Do everything without murmuring or misgivings . . . . loyal to the word of life, to be my pride on the day of Christ, show-

ing that I have not run in vain or labored in vain " (Phil.
2:14-16). Paul would therefore have run in vain and missed the
crown given by Christ, if the communities failed to be what
they should have been. The Apostle's work must not be done
merely in good faith. It must have regard to the whole church
of God and its future.

³*But not even my companion Titus, though he was a Greek,
was forced to submit to circumcision.*

The discussion was about the validity of the law. Paul does not
mention here the basic matters spoken about, but he anticipates
the practical conclusions. Titus, who was uncircumcised, was
not forced to submit to circumcision. The apostles did not order
him to take over this Jewish practice. He is therefore not obliged
to obey the law. The Christian is free with regard to the law.

⁴*For the sake of the intruders, the false Christians who had made
their way in to spy upon the freedom which we possess in Jesus
Christ, in order to be able to enslave us . . .*

False brethren have been introduced into the communities. They
felt their way cautiously. These are Christians who do not deserve
the name of brethren, and what they do is not the Christian way
of brotherly admonition. They play the role of inspectors, and
what is worse, they do it in an underhanded way, like spies. They
cause confusion in the fellowship of the brethren. Thus was the
situation in Antioch: " Certain people came down from Judea
and taught the brethren that if they were not circumcised according to the practice established by Moses, they could not be saved "
(Acts 15:1). Anyone who keeps his brother under surveillance
does not deserve the name of brother.

The object of the false brethren is to reduce the community to slavery. They aim at nothing short of imposing a yoke of servitude on Christians. This of course they do not say openly, but it is what they mean. It follows from the logic of circumcision. This is what Paul explains to the Galatians, among whom false brethren have now intruded. They speak of salvation coming through the law and demand that all should be circumcised. To follow their counsel is to give up one's freedom and subject oneself to slavery.

Our freedom is at stake. We have attained in Christ the status of free men and adult Christians. This means first of all that it is Christ who has bestowed on us this freedom (5:1, 13). It also means that all who are incorporated into Christ by baptism (3:26-29) live under the rule of freedom, being children of God by faith. Who would wish to risk this freedom?

⁵we did not yield and submit ourselves for a moment, intent only on upholding the truth of the gospel for you.

Paul did not yield. Having expressed his contempt for the false brethren by a sharp characterization of their role, Paul now takes up his train of thought again. He did not yield to pressure for the sake of the false brethren, not even for a moment. Though he had subjected Timothy to circumcision before taking him with him on his second missionary journey (Acts 16:3), in the case of Titus he refused to make any concession. Here in Jerusalem the truth of the gospel was at stake. It was otherwise in the case of Timothy. There was a serious debate in Jerusalem. The false brethren pleaded in vain. The apostles did not demand the circumcision of Titus. They decided in favor of Paul, who had maintained his position unbendingly throughout the affair.

The happy result is that the truth of the gospel remains inviolate among the Galatians and indeed among all gentile Christians. Paul had not merely followed his conscience in the debate. He had also had the good of his communities in mind. They were to remain free from the burden of the law. That is why he cannot permit the truth of the gospel to be distorted. His gospel is the truth (see 2:14; 5:7), and it is threatened by the demands of the false teachers in Galatia. Paul watches passionately over the message which Christ entrusted to him. It proclaims redemption and liberates from the servitude of the law.

GOSPEL AND APOSTOLATE MET WITH RECOGNITION (2:6–10)

Verses 6-10 form one long sentence into which many thoughts are combined, with only the last verse standing somewhat apart from the rest. The subject is still the agreement reached in Jerusalem. No additional burdens were imposed on Paul, except that he should be mindful of the mother church at Jerusalem, " the poor " (2:10). The authorities, the first apostles, recognized the special grace and call which had been bestowed on Paul to work for the gentiles, and that the same Lord who was working through Peter was working through him. They made a pact with him, " gave him their right hand " (2:9), and divided the mission field among themselves and him.

⁶But as regards the men of repute—what they once were does not matter to me, God pays no heed to personal qualities—these men of repute imposed no further duties on me.

The decision was given by the men of repute, that is, the authorities in Jerusalem, who are recognized and acknowledged as such by all, including Paul.

When speaking of them Paul remarks, before he comes to what he really wants to say, that their " past " does not interest him here. What they may have been once is unimportant now. Even though when preaching the gospel they can point to the

fact that they have known Jesus during his earthly life and con-
versed with him after the resurrection, these personal privileges
cannot be decisive in such a question as is debated here.

God is no respecter of persons. He does not regard the " face,"
that is, the human qualities of a man. If he did, he certainly
would not have called Paul. God accepts Jews and gentiles alike.
It was this impartial God who is welcoming and merciful to all,
whom Jesus made manifest in his conduct, especially when dealing with sinners.

Paul was not charged—and this is of importance for the
Galatians—to add anything to his gospel. God demands faith of
men, not works of the law. Circumcision is not necessary for
salvation; the first apostles in Jerusalem have so decided. Nothing
is changed: the gospel remains the same as Paul has always
preached it.

*7On the contrary, when they saw that the gospel to the uncir-
cumcised had been entrusted to me, like that of the circumcised
to Peter . . .*

What Paul and his companions had to narrate caused the authorities in Jerusalem to see. The Acts of the Apostles gives Paul's
account in the following terms: " Brothers, you know that God
chose me long ago among you "—Peter is speaking—" so that the
gentiles might hear from me the message of the gospel and
believe. And God, who knows the hearts of men, gave testimony
on their behalf by giving the Holy Spirit as he did to us. And he
made no difference between them and us, having cleansed their
hearts by faith " (Acts 15:7-9). The community then listened in
silence, as Barnabas and Paul told of " the great signs and won-
ders which God has wrought through them among the gentiles "

(Acts 15 : 12). Decisions of the church often result from insight into the action of God. Through the experience and the history of the church new knowledge can be arrived at with regard to the faith and its implications.

It is not only recognized in Jerusalem that Paul is an apostle and that he has the gospel. It is also recognized that the gospel for the uncircumcised has been entrusted to him. Paul uses terms here which reflect the Jewish-Christian way of thinking. The term " uncircumcised " for the pagans had a contemptuous ring. When Paul uses it here, the Galatians can recognize that God does not look on them with contempt. He has no respect for personal qualities and calls his new people together out of Jews and gentiles to form the church.

The gospel for the gentiles is entrusted to Paul. God gave it to him to guard carefully and the Apostle must preserve it inviolate. He may add nothing to it and he must preach it without omissions.

The gospel was entrusted by God to Paul as it had been to Peter. There is no difference in the contents of the message, which is the same on the lips of all the apostles. The difference is in the field of operations, though even this is not divided up as a matter of principle. On the other hand, it was not just by accident that each found himself in a different field. Peter, an inhabitant of Palestine, has stood at the center of the Jerusalem community since the first Christian Pentecost. Paul, a Jew of the diaspora, was predestined, so to speak, for the gentile nation. He knows that he has been sent in a special way to the gentiles, and the success of his missionary effort is no slight confirmation of his own sense of vocation. Now the authorities in Jerusalem realize it also. Peter and Paul preach the same gospel, each in his own way and to different groups of men. " So whether it is they or I—this is what we preach, and this is how you have believed " (1 Cor. 15 : 11).

8—for God, who worked in Peter to make him an apostle to the circumcised, worked also in me with regard to the gentiles—

God has worked for the benefit of the two apostles, which is the only explanation of the success of the mission. Their hearers have not accepted the word of God " as though it were the word of men but, as it truly is, as the word of God," as Paul writes to the Thessalonians. And he adds that " in the faithful, it is also efficacious " (1 Thess. 2 : 13). The word of God was accompanied throughout by the divine power (see Acts 5 : 12). Thus God intervenes on behalf of his messengers. The signs point to the election of those in whose favor they are wrought. " For our preaching of the gospel among you took the form not only of words, but of power and the works of the Holy Spirit " (1 Thess. 1 : 5).

9and when they recognized the grace that is granted me, then James, Cephas, and John, the acknowledged pillars, gave Barnabas and myself their right hand in fellowship: we should go to the gentiles and they to the circumcised.

The apostles did not merely see that the gospel was entrusted to Paul. They also recognized the grace given to him, the grace which he had received with his apostolic office. It makes the Apostle what he is : " By the grace of God I am what I am, and his grace was not given to me in vain. In fact, I labored more than any of them, though not I, but the grace of God which was with me " (1 Cor. 15 : 10). When God confers a charge and an office, he also gives the strength which is needed to exercise them.

The three who are acknowledged to be the pillars of the community now give Paul and his companions from Antioch their hands. James is mentioned first. He seems to have been highly revered by Paul's opponents in Galatia, and he had a special position in the primitive community. Peter and John also have a leading position in the accounts of the Jerusalem community given in the Acts. The three leading apostles thus confirm the fact that Paul participates in the one office, that of apostle of Christ, and thus the decision is given in favor of Paul. The three pillars act for the whole church. Just like the name " Rock " (Peter, Cephas), the expression " pillars " presupposes the image of the church as a building. The church is supported by its pillars, and without them it would collapse. Paul and his apostolic office are fully in accord with them.

The three apostles gave Paul and his companions their right hand. They made a pact with one another. The common fellowship of the apostles is given clear expression here. The peaceful agreement arrived at is that Paul and Barnabas should go to the gentiles, while the three others go to the Jews. This decision recognizes the fact that Paul is an apostle. It also means that he shares the fellowship of the other apostles. But the decision itself means more than just a demarcation of fields of labor. It indicates the basic objects of the work in each case. This does not mean that they work peacefully in different departments, but that they work together at the same work. The distribution of pastoral work is not to cause divisions, but to promote the work common to all.

[10]*Only they wished us to remember the poor. And this was the very thing which I was most anxious to do.*

The agreement left Paul and his gentile Christians with a debt of gratitude to pay. They were to be mindful of the poor. No other demands were made upon Paul beyond the fact that he should remember the poor of Jerusalem. Who are these poor? They are the poor of the primitive community in Jerusalem, who were particularly numerous. But it must also be remembered that the members of this primitive community looked upon themselves as the poor to whom the Lord had assigned the kingdom of heaven (Mt. 5:3; Lk. 6:20). And in fact, when collecting money among the gentile Christians, Paul never bases his appeal on the poverty of Jerusalem but on the fact that the church took its start in Jerusalem. " Macedonia and Achaia have determined to make a collection for the ' the poor ' of the saints in Jerusalem. They have determined, and rightly, for they are in their debt. For if they shared with the gentiles their spiritual possessions, these are bound to furnish them with material things " (Rom. 15:26f.).

Paul made every effort to pay this debt. He knew that Jerusalem made him no contribution as regards the gospel. So he is not also obliged to Jerusalem in the sense that the gospel message had been brought to him from there. But Jerusalem remains the city of the primitive community. Historically speaking, it is the homeland of the church, the mother church of all churches. The temporal gifts sent by the gentile Christians testify to their grateful links with Jerusalem and hence to the unity of the church of Christ.

Third Proof: Paul Upheld the Truth of his Gospel even in Face of Peter (2:11–21)

After Paul had successfully maintained the truth of his gospel in the decisive debate at Jerusalem (2:1-10), another grave situation arose

which enables Paul to show how his gospel was also respected by
Peter.

PETER'S BEHAVIOR IN ANTIOCH WAS NOT CONSISTENT
(2:11–13)

[11]*But when Cephas came to Antioch, I opposed him to his face,
because he was blameable.* [12]*For before certain persons came from
James, he used to eat with the gentiles. But when these arrived,
he withdrew and kept himself aloof, being afraid of the party of
the circumcision.*

Paul resisted the attack to which Peter's behavior gave occasion.
He " opposed him to his face." He called Peter to account in
Antioch.

There is a sort of headline over this brief account—that Peter
was at fault. His conduct had already condemned him even
before Paul challenged him. A teacher's doctrine does not stand
condemned if the teacher's conduct is contrary to his words. But
the teacher is blameable if his words and deeds are not in accord.

How was Peter at fault? He was guilty of an inconsistency
which was dangerous for the church. While in Antioch, he had
been accustomed to sitting down at table, which included the
eucharistic meal, along with the gentile Christians. Now some
Jewish Christians appear, commissioned by James, and Peter
begins to feel anxiety. Out of fear of the Jewish Christians, he
gradually withdraws from the company of the gentile Christians.
He held himself aloof. In doing so, he contradicts in practice
the profound meaning of the Eucharist, which unites all men
in Christ.

Peter acts from timidity, not from conviction. Paul and
Barnabas could take the company of gentile Christians for

granted, but perhaps it was not so easy for Peter. The result is that in his timidity, he has more consideration for the envoys from Jerusalem than is permissible in the cause of the gospel. The way churchmen actually behave and the decisions of church politics are often interpreted by the faithful as directives on doctrine and principles. That is the way things go. Paul sees the trend and resists it vigorously.

[13]*And the other Jewish Christians fell into line with his hypocrisy, so that even Barnabas was carried away and acted as hypocritically as the others.*

Peter's behavior affects the other Jewish Christians, and they conform to his insincere way of acting. These Jewish Christians belong to the community of Antioch. It is taken for granted from the start that the envoys from James kept themselves aloof from the gentile Christians. Peter's example sets the fashion since he is looked up to in his authoritative position. Example is more effective than the words in which a matter of principle is taught.

Even Barnabas, who is accustomed to living with gentile Christians, is swept along by the tide of hypocrisy. The unity of the Antioch church is seriously endangered. The same process was going on at Antioch which now threatens the church of Galatia. Jewish-Christian agitators are undermining the communities by their dishonesty and are even distorting the truth of the gospel.

PAUL CALLED PETER TO ACCOUNT (2:14)

It may have been sufficient at Antioch to denounce the inconsistency in Peter's behavior (2:14). For the Galatians, the Apostle

must expound the principles which are only touched on here
(2 : 15-21).

*14But when I saw that they were not acting straightforwardly
with regard to the truth of the gospel, I said to Cephas in front
of all: If you, in spite of being a Jew, live like a gentile and not
like a Jew, how can you try to force the gentiles to follow
Jewish customs?*

Paul saw clearly what was happening. The Judaizers were not
acting straightforwardly. Their conduct was crooked with regard
to the truth of the gospel. Their behavior cannot be excused by
pleading that Peter still preached the same gospel as a matter
of principle. In his actual practice Peter was denying the gospel.
He has as it were been limping instead of marching straight
ahead uprightly. He has denied in practice the unity of Jews
and Christians to which Christ has opened up the way for mankind. Christ " has made both one, destroying the barrier of
enmity that stood between them like a wall, and abolishing in
his flesh all the precepts and the rulings of the law " (Eph.
2 : 14f.). The human race, created anew, is no longer divided by
the law. It is the church which is composed of both Jews and
gentiles.

Paul brings home to Peter the inconsistency of his behavior.
Though Peter is a Jew born and bred, he has not been following the Jewish way of life, which he has renounced on principle. As an apostle of Christ and a " new man," he is not
bound by the law. Peter is fully aware of this. When he gave up
his Christian way of life at Antioch, he was contradicting himself, and at the same time, forcing the gentile Christians to adopt
Jewish customs. If they wished to eat once more at the same

table as Peter, they would have to submit to circumcision and all the precepts of the law. Peter, how can you do a thing like that? How can you act so shortsightedly? How can you put such burdens on the gentile Christians and throw them into such confusion?

Paul did not ask these questions in private. He put them publicly, before the whole assembled community. Since Peter had given open scandal, the matter had to be cleared up publicly, before the whole church. No misplaced respectfulness could have been allowed to interfere. Paul had the courage to clarify the situation in a public speech.

No Righteousness through the Law (2:15-21)

Verses 15-21 appear at first sight to be the speech directed against Peter which Paul delivered " before all " at Antioch. But they are primarily to be understood as a presentation of the fundamental truth which was being denied in practice at Antioch. The false teachers clearly go beyond this in Galatia, where they call in question the fundamental truth of the gospel (1:6f., 9). Hence the " discourse " which we read here is not a reproduction of what Paul had said at Antioch. It gives the principles which were endangered at Antioch, and which were also threatened in the communities of Galatia. Finally, they must also be pondered by today's readers.

[15] *We ourselves are Jews by birth and not heathen sinners.* [16a]*But we know that one is not justified by the works of the law, but by faith in Jesus Christ . . .*

To understand this passage and indeed the whole of the epistle, we must understand exactly what " justification," " to declare just," and " to make just " mean. These words are not ordinarily part of our religious vocabulary, they are primarily juridical terms. In the Jewish religion of Jesus' day, justification was the key-word for the relationship between sinful man and the holy God. The great question was : How can I appear just before God's judgment and be declared just by him? How can I face God as a sinner? Paul takes over these terms but gives them a new content. Above all, he does not merely think of the last judgment but of our present life on earth, and he teaches that man is already made just (" justified ") by God, even at present, through the death of Jesus. Justification takes place even in this life, really and effectively, so that the sinner is turned into a just man, sin is actually removed, and grace bestowed. The " old man " is transformed into a new man. It follows that the question of justification must become central in the Apostle's preaching : it will be the parting of the ways for the Old and New Testament. Our whole life will be decided by the answer to the question : Am I myself already justified, and if so, how must I live?

Paul knows that he is at one with Peter and the other Jewish Christians in being Jews by birth. That in itself is a distinction. The Jews have the privilege of possessing much that others lack : " Sonship of God conferred on them, the majesty of God's presence, the covenants, the legislation, the liturgy, and the promises "; finally, " the fathers " and the fact that " Christ is descended from them according to the flesh " (Rom. 9 : 4f.).

In contrast to the Jews, the heathen are sinners. Paul is not speaking ironically here when he uses an expression which corresponds to Jewish ways of thinking. The heathen not merely fail to fulfill the law. They do not even know it. The Jew knew that zeal for the fulfillment of the law was impossible among the heathen, and he was proud of his spiritual possessions.

But there is a truth that runs counter to this privilege of the

Jews: no one is justified by the works of the law. For " all have
sinned and are without the glory of God. They are made just,
without any merit of their own, by the grace of God through
the redemption accomplished in Christ Jesus " (Rom. 3:23f.).
The works demanded by the law are powerless to make a man
righteous before God and to enable him to face God's judgment.

On the contrary, it is only through faith in Christ Jesus that
a man can be justified. This faith, which draws its force from the
redemptive act of Christ, is the means of justification. Righteousness cannot result from the works of the law but only from
faith. This faith is the act of confessing Christ Jesus. It means
saying " yes " to Jesus the Messiah, to his person, his work, his
word. Jesus is God's envoy, the bringer of salvation, with whose
coming faith became the saving power (3:23-25). The Jewish
way to salvation is thereby closed, the law is ended as the way to
salvation.

[16bc] . . . *so we too have believed in Jesus Christ, in order that we*
might be justified through faith in Christ and not through the
works of the law. For " no one will be justified through the
works of the law."

Paul now reaches the climax. Although we are Jews, we have
believed. We acknowledged Jesus the Messiah at baptism, and
since then we have professed our faith in him. We adopted at
baptism the Christian way of life and we continue to live by it.
Faith is both the decision once made in the past and the life of
faith in the present. We have taken the way of faith towards
salvation, and justification awaits us.

For the goal of the act of faith is the hope of being made
righteous. When these Jews became Christians at baptism, they

aimed at being made just through faith in Christ. They knew as they were being baptized that this goal could not be reached by means of the works of the law. With this admission, they gave up their Jewish religion.

The Book of Psalms had already indicated to the Jews that no one is justified in the sight of God. Paul quotes this text of scripture very freely (Ps. 143:2). He underlines the sinfulness of all men by using (in the Greek) the strong expression " no flesh." And he also inserts the words, which are decisive in the present context, " through the works of the law." For all mankind lived by the works of the law. Gentiles as well as Jews wished to make themselves righteous in God's sight by their achievements (see 4:10 below). But at the moment that the Jews in question became Christians, they rejected these efforts as self-righteousness and took the way of faith. Paul keeps to this way, and the Jewish Christians should likewise stand by their Christian decision.

¹⁷But if we ourselves, as we strove to be justified in Christ, were discovered also to be sinners, is not Christ then the servant of sin? Far from it!

Paul is now in the middle of the theological discussion. He foresees the objection that it is incredible, indeed, almost a blasphemy, that Christ should appear to be the servant of sin, as what Paul has said might suggest. For justification by faith seems to make Christ an abettor of sin. The intervention takes the form, apparently, of a pious objection which is intent on guarding the honor of the Messiah. For it is true after all: if even the Jews, just as much as the gentiles, wished to be justified when they made the act of faith, then they too must have been sinners. And in that case—the objection goes on—Christ has undoubtedly favored sin; he is in the service of sin and not in the service of righteousness! It is the same misgiving as was voiced by the pious Jews who criticized Jesus' contacts with sinners. " When certain doctors of the law from among the Pharisees saw that he was eating along with tax gatherers and sinners, they said to his disciples: ' Why is he eating along with tax gatherers and sinners?' And Jesus heard them and said to them: ' Those who are well have no need of a doctor, only those who are ill. I am not come to call the just, but sinners ' " (Mk. 2:16f.).

Paul rejects decisively the objection based on piety. The Apostle has understood the will of the Messiah exactly and essentially, and he holds firmly to his assertion. Then he goes on to try to give the theological reasons for his teaching.

[18]*For if I try to build up once more what I have pulled down, then I prove myself a transgressor.*

Paul now answers the pious criticism and gives his reason for rejecting it. He begins by taking up the action of those who reject justification by Christ and depict it as a transgression. He speaks here in the first person, but he is not referring to his own case. He uses this lively style to speak for any Jewish Christian, which he does also in verses 19-20.

Paul takes the case of a Jew who has " pulled down " the law, building it up once more. By believing and being baptized, he has dismissed the law with all its demands and achievements. He has given up thinking of the performance of the law as the way to righteousness. And now he does something that no one would have expected: he sets up the law again, and tries to make it once more the valid and effective way to righteousness.

Such an undertaking is not just inconsistent. To attempt it is to display oneself as a transgressor. It is not Christ who is the servant of sin, but the Jewish Christian who upholds once more the validity of the law. Through the cross of Christ, this world and its principles of law have been crucified and eliminated (6:14). Anyone who revives this principle and lets it dominate his life is a transgressor. He makes himself a breaker of the commandments, from whose fulfillment he expects salvation.

In explaining in this way his dismissal of the objection, Paul is thinking primarily of Peter's case. He and the Jewish Christians who followed him were on the way to becoming such transgressors. The Galatians too, although gentile Christians, are on the point of making achievements the way to salvation (4:8-10). Every Christian is in danger of being enticed to follow the way of the performance of the law once more. If he does so, he will not be righteous before God, but will prove himself a transgressor.

[19]*For through the law I died to the law, that I might live for God. I am crucified along with Christ.*

The second and positive reason for Paul's " far from it!" consists of an explanation of what happened to the lower nature in baptism. If one is aware of this, one will understand that Christ is not the servant of sin.

The Christian has died to the law. He was once the living victim on which the baneful power of the law could exercise itself. But now he is no longer at the disposal of the law. He is just as much out of the reach of the law and its claims as if he were dead. The law can no longer count on him.

The Christian lives for God. This is the power who rules his life, for whom he lives, towards whom he has orientated himself. His eyes are no longer fixed on the law but on God. Just as Christ died to sin once and for all, so too the Christian is dead to sin. And just as the risen Lord lives for God, so too it is true of all who were crucified along with Christ in baptism: "So too you must look on yourselves as dead to sin, but living for God, in Christ Jesus our Lord" (Rom. 6:11). The new life of the baptized brings with it a new orientation, which is directed solely and immediately to God.

How are we to understand Paul's declaration that the baptized have died through the law? Has the law killed us? Yes, the law is in fact the author of our death. Just as we can say that it was through sin that Christ died on the cross, and that he has conquered sin by his death, so too Paul can say: "Christ has ransomed us from the curse of the law, by becoming himself a curse for us" (3:13). Christ was crucified by the power of the law, which exercised its might by the will of God when killing Christ, but still acted unjustly. And therefore the cross not only removed Christ from this world but the faithful too, who were crucified with Christ. They have been withdrawn from the sphere of the law's influence.

The effects of Christ's death on the cross are imparted to man in baptism, where he was crucified along with Christ. He became "united to Christ by the likeness to his death" (Rom. 6:5). He was buried. But the object of this burial along with Christ was that we, "being raised from the dead like Christ," should likewise "live a new life" (Rom. 6:4).

[20]I live now, but it is no longer I, it is Christ who lives in me. As far as I live this bodily life, I live in the faith of the Son of God, who loved me and delivered himself for me.

The rejection of the reproach that Paul presents Christ as the servant of sin is now further justified by the life which the baptized live.

Christ lives in me. The baptized may say this. The life of Christ is so dominant in the Christian that he can no longer ascribe the conduct of his life to his own nature. " It is no longer I " who live. It is no longer true that he " leads " a life of which his achievements are the mainspring. The life of the baptized is determined by Christ, who works and reigns in him. But Christ dwells in Christians through the Spirit. " You are not in the flesh but in the Spirit, if indeed the Spirit of God dwells in you. Anyone who does not possess the Spirit of Christ does not belong to him " (Rom. 8:9). Justification in Christ does not merely bring about the death of the old man, it creates a new one, whose person is now the place where Christ lives. Hence the Apostle can say : " Christ is life for me " (Phil. 1:21).

But Paul is aware that he is still living " in the flesh." The Christian has not yet put off his earthly, fleshly body, and his human life on earth still goes on. But " though we live in the flesh, we do not give battle as the flesh would direct. For the weapons of our fight are not fleshly " (2 Cor. 10:3f.). The battle station of the Christian life is determined by the fact that the baptized already belongs to the new age and is a new creation, but at the same time still lives in the flesh, which is part of the old, doomed world. Thus when Paul speaks of the flesh, he does not mean primarily the material body, but the tragic state of the old world which has been crucified by the death of Christ.

The earthly life of the Christian is led in faith in the Son of God. Faith is the new mode of being which corresponds to the new life. Faith does not merely lead up to a new life. It embraces it, accompanies and supports it. The new life indeed cannot be directly known. It is hidden. " You are dead, and your life is hidden with Christ in God. When Christ our life is revealed, you will also be revealed with him in glory " (Col. 3:3f.).

The faith of the baptized is not just general confidence in the mercy of God. It is faith in the Son of God, whose action has made God the Father visible. The action of the Son demonstrates his love for *me* and his self-dedication for *me*. Thus in the light of faith I see my life as a gift of Christ's love. It is a grace bestowed through the self-sacrifice of the Son of God. My life no longer appears to me as something that I can plan on my own and direct independently.

The Christian who ponders this truth and makes it his own is truly not engaged in making Christ the servant of sin! He knows that Christ serves the glory of the Father. When Christ justifies the sinner, the sinner receives his life anew from the hand of God.

[21]*I do not discard the grace of God. For if righteousness comes through the law, then Christ has died in vain.*

Paul closes the first part of his letter with a statement based on the fact, undeniable even by the Apostle's opponents, that Christ's death cannot have been wasted. But if the law had been capable of bringing about righteousness, Christ would not have needed to die. His death would have been pointless. When the Son of God delivered himself to death, his act cannot have remained fruitless.

Paul emphasizes so forcefully the fact that he does not discard grace that one suspects that he is defending himself against a reproach. This reproach can have been made by the Judaizers around Peter and James. But it may also have been made by Paul's opponents in Galatia. If so, they mean by " grace " the special privileges of Israel, which Paul recounts on other occasions. Paul does not sweep aside the grace of God. But grace for him does not mean the law and the righteousness expected from it, but the new life which can only come through the death of Christ (2:20b).

The Galatians risk losing this grace, when they wish to become just through the law (5:4). But if one eliminates the grace of Jesus Christ and declares that it is unimportant, then Christ has died for nothing—which is impossible. But if this is inconceivable, so too is all righteousness which is based on the works of the law.

RIGHTEOUSNESS COMES FROM FAITH, NOT FROM THE WORKS OF THE LAW (3:1—4:31)

In the first two chapters of the epistle Paul has firmly established his apostolic authority, which had been threatened in Galatia by the accusations of the false teachers. Paul has now proved that he received his apostolate and his gospel directly from Christ. He can now turn to the content of his gospel, which is being distorted by the innovators in Galatia (1:7). That is why, in fact, they are trying to undermine the standing of Paul. The Galatians are not merely to be enticed away from Paul, but from his gospel. This is the real aim of the attack.

Paul now takes up the defense of his message. This is done in two stages. He first appeals to the experience of the Galatians (3:1-5). The converts have themselves had proof of the work of the Holy Spirit. They should therefore bear in mind that they did not receive the Spirit through the works of the law but through the preaching of the faith. It was through Paul's message of the faith alone that they had had "such great experiences" (see 3:4). Therefore, salvation lies along the way of faith, not of law.

But there is another element in Paul's proof. In it he challenges above all the teachers who are disturbing the Christians of Galatia. They are Jewish Christians. They believe in the law as the way of salvation. And Paul argues with them from premises which they acknowledge. He bases his proof on the scripture of the Old Testament. The Old Testament, if properly understood, already clearly points out the way of faith as the way of salvation. This Paul demonstrates by the history of the just man, Abraham. His name gives continuity, as it were, to the proof from scripture which the Apostle then adduces using the method of midrash (3:6—4:31). Abraham and

51

the texts of scripture which speak of him, the progenitor of Israel, point to the way of faith. They tell against the works of the law as a possible way to righteousness.

God himself speaks in the scriptures. They disclose to us God's plan of salvation and the way it will take. Paul takes his stand on scripture not merely because his adversaries do the same and because it is so easy to silence them by such arguments; his main reason is that he does not identify sacred scripture and the law. Scripture remains the word of God in which he addresses us and proclaims his will (Rom. 15:4). But since Christ, the law is no longer valid, and faith has intervened (Gal. 3:23-25). " Christ is the end of the law, bringing righteousness to all who believe " (Rom. 10:4). Taking the example of Abraham, Paul shows that according to the testimony of scripture the law was never a way to righteousness, nor was it meant to be, according to the will of God. Righteousness is granted to men as a gift, because of faith. It is grace, a gift bestowed by God without any merit on the part of man.

Experience Shows that the Spirit Comes from the Preaching of Faith, not From the Works of the Law (3:1-5)

¹ᵃ*What fools you are, you Galatians! How could you have let yourselves be bewitched . . .*

The Apostle had already allowed his proof of his divine mission to turn into an exposition of the main interest of his letter, that righteousness does not come from the law (2:15-21). This shows how much he is preoccupied by this theme and how anxious he is to develop it. But now he has to take it up in view of the Galatians' attitude before he treats it on its own. He addresses them by name—" you stupid Galatians "—and calls them personally to account. He does not plead with them. He pays them no compliments. He tells them that they are fools. But the Apostle seems to be expressing his amazement at the Galatians, whose conduct he cannot understand. The term he uses does not refer to intellectual defects. It does not mean that they are incapable of understanding, but that they do not use their brains. The Galatians fail to see something which they are perfectly well able to see and had every reason to see. They still have not grasped the fact that law and faith are two different things.

What has happened to the Galatians can hardly be attributed to the power of human persuasion; it seems rather that they have been bewitched. Who could have cast his spell over the Galatians? What demonic power has control over them? Paul, the pastor, is dismayed when he thinks of how they once absorbed his own preaching.

[1b]. . . *you before whose eyes Jesus Christ was publicly depicted as the crucified?*

The conduct of the Galatians is all the stranger because Christ had been publicly depicted before their eyes. One would have expected that the Galatians would be enthralled by him and that they would have kept him before their eyes forever. For Christ the crucified is an obvious proof of the grace which God bestows upon us. Christ on the cross is the pledge of the righteousness which we are receiving from God. To keep the picture of the crucified before the eyes is to be preserved from all folly, and to avoid the mistake of expecting justification from one's own efforts.

Paul recalls his missionary preaching among the Galatians. It is significant that for him it meant making Christ known as the crucified. Jesus Christ has been displayed in due course to the

Galatians, like a proclamation which has been posted up publicly. Paul sees in the preaching of the missionary the official and public execution of his duties as a herald. He proclaims the message which his divine master has charged him to deliver. Here he gives its essence in a few short words: " Jesus Christ the crucified " (see 1 Cor. 1 : 23). For Paul, of course, the message of the crucifixion and death of Jesus also includes the resurrection. The resurrection is the side of the death on the cross which is turned towards us. In his capacity as a missionary, therefore, Paul was not interested in giving an impressive and moving picture of the crucified, but in proclaiming him solemnly as the Lord, as God had charged him to do.

This was done *publicly* by Paul. A proclamation is given full publicity, so that everyone can see it. No one can help noticing it. It may be disregarded, but it cannot be missed. And that is how Paul preached. The unnamed false teachers, on the other hand, seem to have practiced their " magic " in secret. Their agitation went on behind closed doors while Paul made his proclamations public. It may very well be that Christians who receive obscure " messages " by devious ways may find them more fascinating than the public preaching of the Church.

²I should like you to tell me this one thing: Was it from the works of the law that you received the Spirit, or from the faith that was preached to you?

Paul has really only one question to put to the Galatians, and the answer to it should be enlightening. They are all acquainted with the Christian experience of the possession of the Spirit. They received the Spirit in baptism. They have the " first fruits of the Spirit " (Rom. 8 : 23), they are " endowed with the Spirit "

(Gal. 6:1). Paul singles out the fact of their possessing the Spirit because the Holy Spirit is the greatest gift of God's love towards us.

How did Christians come to possess the Spirit? Paul signals two possible ways. The decision in favor of the second is so obvious that Paul does not need to give any answer at all: " from the faith that was preached " by the Apostle. When the Galatians received the Spirit at baptism, they had not performed any works of the law beforehand, they had only accepted the preaching of the faith. Elsewhere (Rom. 10:8), Paul calls his preaching the " word of faith." He goes on to explain that the response of the human heart to the message of the cross consists of faith in the resurrection of Christ; this faith leads to justification (see Rom. 10:9f.).

³Are you then so foolish? Have you begun in the Spirit, to end now in the flesh?

Paul continues his insistent questioning: Do you then wish to be so foolish? The Galatians began their Christian existence in the Spirit, who was imparted to them at baptism. He dwells in the baptized, but it can also be said that the baptized dwell in him. The Spirit is the power of God, which creates man anew in baptism and raises him from the dead at the end. But the Spirit is also the " wind " which " impels " the ship of Christian life, if only the Christian lets himself be impelled by it (see Rom. 8:14). By the help of the Spirit, the Christian must " put to death the activities of the lower nature " (Rom. 8:13), otherwise he misses life's goal.

The Galatians are in danger of ending in the flesh. They do not draw the consequences which follow from being crucified with

Christ (2:19). If they wish to have circumcision performed upon their body, they are doing something which makes them citizens of an antiquated and doomed world. Then they will end in death instead of in life. They cannot find the fulfillment which they would like to have from the law.

⁴Have you had such great experiences in vain—if indeed they were in vain?

Paul cannot believe that the Galatians have received the gift of the Spirit in vain. Such a mighty experience cannot be devoid of effect. The Apostle himself believes firmly in the creative power of the Spirit, who displays himself in man even after baptism. When he says so here, it is to encourage his menaced Christians to make progress in the Spirit along the saving way of faith.

⁵So, he who furnishes you with the Spirit and works miracles among you—does he do it by reason of the works of the law or of the preaching of faith?

The final question contrasts once more the two possible ways to righteousness. Paul puts the two expressions, " works of the law " and " preaching " of faith, in an emphatic position at the end of the sentence. Now the question to be considered points to the present experience of the efficacy of the Spirit in the communities. God is still bestowing the Spirit on the Galatians at the present moment. They experience it in the extraordinary effects of the Spirit which are known as charismatic gifts. They experience it in the works of divine power and the signs which they see taking place among them, in exorcisms and in miracles of healing. The messianic age which is beginning is manifested in all these things.

They are a confirmation of the gospel which the Apostle proclaimed as the envoy of God. This impressive presence of the Spirit does not come from the works of the law. The Galatians can themselves bear witness: it comes from the preaching of the faith. Before it was heard among them, there were no charismatic gifts. But with the preaching of the salvific way of faith and with the acceptance of the message in faith the " accompanying signs " also arrived (see Mk. 16:17. 20).

Paul does not need to sum up the result of his questioning in a set answer. It is obvious to anyone who thinks. The reception of the Spirit and the activity of the Spirit do not come from the works of the law. They come from faith. But since the Spirit is the pledge of perfected righteousness, righteousness comes from faith.

The Old Testament Confirms the Gospel of Paul (3:6—4:31)

The Blessing of Abraham Comes through Faith (3:6-14)

THE FAITHFUL ARE CHILDREN OF ABRAHAM AND ARE BLESSED (3:6-9)

⁶*It is true: " Abraham believed God, and it was reckoned to him as righteousness" (Gen. 15:6). ⁷You can be sure, therefore, that those who believe are children of Abraham.*

The scripture proof which Paul now gives for his gospel of righteousness through faith begins with the verdict of sacred scripture on the ancestor of Israel. God had promised Abraham that his descendants would be as numerous as the stars of heaven

(Gen. 15:5). Though, humanly speaking, Abraham could no longer expect a son from his wife Sarah, he believed the promise which God had made him. He believed in the creative power of God which knows no bounds, and hence he could also believe in the promises of God. The attitude of Abraham was expressed in his act of faith, and this faith, according to the testimony of scripture, made Abraham just before God.

Judaism had not failed to note the faith of the patriarch. But it considered this faith primarily as the individual acts through which Abraham was supposed to have accomplished the whole law. They also spoke of being children of Abraham in a way which meant more than just being descended from him. A true son of Abraham was one who had fulfilled the whole law by his exertions. Paul's attitude was quite different.

Paul does not mean that Abraham's faith was reckoned to him in the way in which positive efforts are toted up. God does not, as it were, keep an account book for each man in which all his achievements are entered so that they can be added up eventually to the sum total of " righteousness." God looks rather to the fundamental act of man whereby he says " yes " to God's promise and God's claims. This is what scripture knows as " faith," and it is this faith that God demands of man. For such faith is the acknowledgement of God as God. This faith produces the obedience which makes man respond to the demands of his divine Lord.

Paul tells us then that we can be sure that those who believe are children of Abraham. He calls believers " men of faith," meaning men who live by faith. They and only they can claim the honored title of children of Abraham. They are akin to Abraham, whose faith inspired him to trust God and follow him. It is not those who live by the works of the law who merit the name of children of Abraham, but those who are " men of faith " like Abraham.

*But since scripture foresaw that God would make the gentiles righteous through faith, it announced the gospel beforehand to Abraham, saying, " All nations will be blessed in you" (Gen. 12 : 3). *Thus those who believe are blessed along with that man of faith, Abraham.*

Another quotation from scripture confirms what Paul has just said. Scripture foresaw that God would make the gentiles righteous. Paul sees scripture as something living and active, not just as a lifeless text. God himself speaks in it. It could, therefore, foresee what was now happening to the gentiles, and already announce to Abraham what God was doing today: blessing all nations in Abraham and making them righteous.

Thus Paul was not the first to bring the good news for the gentiles. It began as early as the promise which said that the blessing bestowed on Abraham would also be bestowed on the heathen nations. Abraham already heard the gospel of the blessing of the heathens. Abraham had believed this evangelical promise. God justifies the heathens too when they, like Abraham, put their faith in God.

From his second scripture text Paul draws the conclusion that those who with Abraham make faith the basis of their life, are also with Abraham bearers of the blessing. They are not just children of Abraham; they also share the great blessing which God bestowed upon Abraham.

At the end of the verse, Paul stresses once more that this Abraham is a man of faith. Abraham enjoys the blessing and passes it on, not because of performing the law, but insofar as he believes God.

TO LIVE BY ACCOMPLISHMENT OF LAWS IS TO BE UNDER A CURSE (3:10–12)

[10]*For all who take their stand on the works of the law are under a curse, since it was written: " Anyone who does not abide by all the precepts in the book of the law and fails to carry them out shall be accursed "* (Deut. 27:26).

The decision to be taken involves choosing between life and death, blessing and curse. Paul is not content with showing only the positive aspect of the blessing which believers receive along with Abraham. He must also show them that it necessarily involves a decisive choice one way or the other. The only alternative to the blessing is a curse; there is no third way. Anyone who bases his existence on the works of the law and makes them the mainspring of his action stands under a curse.

This holds good universally for all who rely on works of the law. It is impossible to profess one's faith in the law and at the same time to profess one's faith in Christ. For anyone who tries for righteousness through the law detaches himself from Christ (5:4). Anyone who thinks that achievements in terms of the law can lead to righteousness has renounced his allegiance to Christ. He no longer wants to have his righteousness as a gift from the hands of God; he scorns the grace which comes through Christ.

With regard to the curse which inevitably comes upon the pious legalist, Paul also recalls a text of scripture which he understands as follows. God's curse falls upon everyone who does not persevere in the matter of fulfilling the demands of the law. If he fails in any one commandment, he is placed under a curse, because he should fulfill the whole law. Any one failure means that the law is disregarded and is bound to bring down the curse with which transgressors are threatened. Thus anyone who lives under the law and builds his life on the works it demands is always under the menace of the curse. He acts from fear. He acts to escape the curse.

Paul first used scripture to show that the pious legalist lives under a curse. Now he returns once more to the question of the way of salvation. He has already answered the question indirectly by referring to Abraham's faith (3:6). Now he answers the question directly, though at first negatively.

¹¹But it is clear that no one is just before God through the law. For " the just will live by faith " (Hab. 2:4). *¹²But the law is not " by faith," since it says: " He that accomplishes it shall live by it "* (Lev. 18:5).

No one is just before God through the law, as must be clear to all who have followed the argument up to this point. The curse pronounced on those who rely on the works of the law could only be averted if its subjects could become just before God. But that is precisely where the law does not help.

Scripture points out the true way to righteousness when it says that the just man receives his life from faith. In the original Hebrew of the text, the prophet Habakkuk speaks of the " steadfastness " which is the just man's assurance of life. When Paul uses the word " faith," it has overtones of the steadfastness of the man who knows that the only safeguard of his life is the fact that he abides by God's word and work. Through his faith he receives righteousness, and this in turn enables him to survive God's judgment and so enter into life.

But is not this faith itself an achievement? Paul rejects the Jewish view that faith should be considered as a meritorious achievement. For if it were a work which gained merit, it would be quite compatible with the legal way of salvation. Paul denies this flatly. The law is not " from faith," and it has nothing in common with faith. Its origin is not to be sought in faith and it lives in a different world where what counts is what men do and achieve (see 3 : 10b). It ascribes a life-giving quality to the work of man accomplished in accordance with the law.

Writing within the framework of the law, at the time when the law was in force, Moses could say : " The man who practices the righteousness based on the law shall gain life by it " (Rom. 10:5). He promised life as the reward of the doer of the law, or of the actions by which he fulfilled the law. But faith is a different story. " The righteousness which comes from faith speaks as follows : . . . The word is close to you, in your mouth and in your heart, the word of faith which we preach " (Rom. 10:6, 8). When a man lives within the sphere of the law, there can be no question of faith.

In Christ the Blessing of Abraham Came to the Faithful (3:13–14)

[13]*Christ has ransomed us from the curse of the law by becoming a curse for us, for it is written: " Accursed is everyone who is hanged upon a tree " (Deut. 21:23) . . .*

The Apostle finally discloses the positive action of God which renders it possible to be righteous before God : Christ has ransomed us. This is what opens up the way for the blessing which is given to the faithful. When Paul speaks of being ransomed by Christ, he is picturing the ransoming of a slave, which has some significant connotations. First, it means that a man is transferred from the bondage of slavery to the emancipation of freedom. Second, it means that there is someone who pays the ransom. Paul takes up this image and develops it as follows: first he depicts the servitude of man, then the way in which Christ effected his ransom, and finally, in the following verse (3:14) he indicates the two-fold aim of this ransom. These statements are not made in general terms. By using the word " us " twice, Paul reminds the Galatians that they also are among those whom Christ set free.

We were under the curse. Whether we were Jews or gentiles, we had passed all our days under the law, and therefore under the curse. Our life was doomed to death because the law brought the curse upon us. We lived in real slavery. The ransom through Christ was effected by his death on the cross, which Paul renders with the words: " By becoming a curse for us." In the crucifixion the law had spent its force against the Messiah of God; Christ was condemned and executed according to the law. Scripture says that a man hanged in this way is accursed. Thus it was clear from the crucifixion that the curse of the law was displayed in the crucified. Paul carefully avoids saying that Christ himself was accursed, for it was not his person that came under the curse.

On the contrary, he became a curse for us. This need not only mean " for our benefit." It must also mean " instead of us," representing us in whom the curse of the law was not in fact made manifest. So too it is said that God " made him, who was free from sin, to be sin for us " (2 Cor. 5:21). He is not a sinner, but he bore the sins of the world. He is not accursed, but he rescued us from the curse of the law, by himself becoming the portrayal of this curse.

14. . . . so that the blessing of Abraham should reach the nations in Christ Jesus, and we receive the promised Spirit through faith.

The emancipation brought by Christ opened up the way for two events in the history of salvation in accordance with the intention of Christ who ransomed us. The blessing of Abraham can now be extended to the nations in the person of Jesus the Messiah. Hitherto the curse of the law had prevented the realization of the blessing promised to Abraham, but now the way lies open for the blessing of Abraham to reach the nations.

The blessing comes to all mankind in Christ Jesus through his redemptive act. But the " in Christ " may also be understood in the sense that Christ himself represents and embodies the blessing of Abraham. He who meets Christ in the form of the gospel is himself blessed by God. Believers are " blessed along with Abraham who believed " (3:9). Hence the promise to Abraham is being fulfilled and becoming a reality, since the redemptive act of Christ. We, as Paul says speaking of the Galatians and himself, participated in this salvific event by receiving the promised Spirit through faith. The Spirit, who is the Spirit of Jesus Christ (4:6), has come to us with Christ. The previous age, that of the law, was characterized by sin and death, but the characteristic of the new messianic age is the Spirit of Christ. Paul can say to the men of this new age: " The law of the Spirit which gives life in Christ Jesus has freed you from the law of sin and death " (Rom. 8:2). " Where the Spirit of the Lord is, there is freedom " (2 Cor. 3:17).

It was through faith that we received the Spirit of the Lord. Paul puts these words in an emphatic position at the end of the section, which had begun with the text of scripture about the faith of Abraham. It was Abraham's faith which made him just before God. When we received the blessing of Abraham, the Holy Spirit, the gift came by means of faith. Christ disclosed to us the way of faith. Faith in fact came with Christ (3:25). Abraham believed in the promise, and we believe that the promise was fulfilled in Christ.

2. The Heritage of Abraham is Linked up with Christ (3:15–29)

The previous section (3:6-14) showed faith as the mediator of the blessing of Abraham, and the next makes it clear that the promised heritage belongs to Christ. Faith is here contrasted with the law, and both are described as objective powers. The role which the law played in history is disclosed (3:19-25). Baptism is shown to be the sacramental foundation of faith (3:26-29).

AN EXAMPLE SHOWS THAT THE LAW CANNOT INVALIDATE THE PROMISE TO ABRAHAM (3:15–18)

15Brethren, I use an example from ordinary life: A valid human testament cannot be set aside or added to.

With a friendly form of address, Paul now announces an illustration taken from everyday life. He chooses his example from the juridical sphere. Just as Jesus presupposed a certain harmony between earthly happenings and the divine order of salvation when he drew his parables from the world of creation and the

everyday life of men, so too Paul is convinced that the works of
God are not totally different from the works of men.

The example is used to trace the relationship between promise
and law. When someone has made a testament which is valid in
law, no one can nullify it or add new clauses to it. As the final
valid declaration of the testator's will, it is inviolate. God made
such a testament in favor of Abraham; he made him promises
which represent his permanent will. For this disposition of God
Paul uses the word current in the Greek Bible for covenant
(*diatheke*). God made a covenant with Israel on Sinai, but he had
already made one with Abraham. The word really means a
(unilateral) disposition, a " testament." For it is God who set up
the " covenant " with man in each case.

*16Now the promises were made to Abraham and to his seed. It
does not say " seeds," as though many were intended, but " and
to your seed," which means only one; and that is Christ.*

Paul refers once more to scripture. The promises of the covenant
with Abraham envisaged not only the patriarch, but also his seed
(Gen. 17:7f.). But " seed " in the singular, according to Paul's
interpretation of the word, is not to be referred to the whole of
Abraham's descendants, the following generations, but to one
descendant of the patriarch, Christ. Christ is the sole heir of the
promises to Abraham. That is the hidden meaning of the word
" seed," which was not seen by the Jews.

*17By this I mean that a testament already declared valid by God
cannot be invalidated by the law which came four hundred and
thirty years later, so that the promise would be nullified.*

Now comes the application of the example which had been given by the Apostle in verse 15. The application was led up to in verse 16, where he pointed out that God made the promises to Abraham and his seed, and endowed them with a testament.

This divine testament, the clear declaration of God's will, cannot be invalidated by the law. A testament is obviously definitive. Since the law was an addition to the promises, and a later one at that, it most certainly cannot nullify the testamentary promises. Here too, Paul contradicts Jewish tradition, which was so preoccupied with the importance of the Sinaitic law that it supposed that Abraham already knew and fulfilled the law. Thus the promises lost their preëminence with regard to the law in Jewish religion. But since the law only came four hundred and thirty years after Abraham it cannot eliminate the testament and the promises to Abraham.

[18]For if the heritage came by the law, it could not come by the promise. Yet God showed himself gracious to Abraham by giving him a promise.

Paul stresses once more that there are no two ways to the heritage of Abraham. The law cannot lead there as well as the promise. The law cannot, as it were, take over the promise and absorb it. Law and promise are two radically different things. They cannot both impart the same benefits of salvation which are contained in the inheritance and the blessing.

The promise of blessing made to Abraham shows that God has determined upon the way of the promise. And this means that the promise cannot be overthrown. It is a proof of God's favor and friendliness, which was given before the law demanded human achievements and produced works.

The Law Has Been our Tutor until Christ (3:19–25)

¹⁹What then was the purpose of the law? It was added for the sake of transgressions, till the seed should come to whom the promise was given. It was laid down by angels and it came through a mediator.

Once Paul had stated that the heritage did not come through the law, the question had to be asked: What is the point of the law and what task did it perform (3:18)? It is the question of the place of the law in the divine history of salvation.

The first answer to the question had really been given earlier when Paul said that the law was an addition which was made four hundred and thirty years later (3:17). He now repeats that it was a later addition. The law is tied to a particular time. It is not one of the things which, according to Jewish belief, already existed before the creation of the world. It is not of the essence of the way of salvation but only an episode in God's dealing with man. The promises were something quite different.

The second answer is that the law was added for the sake of transgressions. This does not mean that it was meant to be a protective barrier against transgression. The view of the Apostle is rather that the law was intended precisely to indicate the presence of sin. According to the divine plan, it was to suggest the very opposite of righteousness. What the law brought about was transgression! "Where there is no law, there is no transgression" (Rom. 4:15b). It is the law which first gives sin its baneful power.

Paul's answer also contains a third point. The time of the law is limited. It was to function only "until the seed came." This seed is Christ (3:16). The promise is for him as it is for Abraham. Hence the promised heritage will belong to those who belong to

Christ, since in Christ they are the seed of Abraham (3:29). Here again Paul contradicts Jewish tradition by denying the permanent duration of the law. The law was to come to an end before history had run its course.

Finally, Paul affirms that the law " was laid down by angels " and that it came " through a mediator." In registering these facts, Paul intends to deprive the law of its standing. He himself had received his gospel directly from God, and Abraham had received the promise directly from God, but the law did not come straight from God. It was imposed on the Israelites by angels, and Moses transmitted it to the people. For the intervention of angels at the giving of the law on Sinai, Paul draws on Jewish tradition. For Moses' mediation, he draws on scripture itself. The promise and the gospel came in quite different ways!

²⁰*A mediator does not intervene where one person is acting; but God is one.*

A general principle rounds off the last part of the answer, the point of which was to demonstrate the inferiority of the law with regard to the gospel and the promise. A mediator is called for when a number of persons on one side treat with the other side, but not when *one* person acts. When one person makes an arrangement with regard to others, he appears in person. But God is one, as all agree. And, therefore, the law cannot come from him (directly). It was instituted by the agency of a group of angels, whose duties were carried on by Moses.

²¹*Is the law then an enemy of the promises of God? Far from it! For if a law had been given which had power to give life, then indeed righteousness would come from the law.*

It might have been deduced from the negative trend of the answer up to this point (3 : 19b-20) that the law was hostile to the divine promises. Paul does not admit this conclusion. The law cannot compete with the promises. For it is a law instituted by angels which came in roundabout ways. But the promises are the promises of God. Thus Paul already indicates his reason for answering in the negative. But he mentions another reason expressly. It is that the law is not lifegiving, and that it does not bring righteousness. If so, it cannot even begin to enter into conflict with the promises. The promises remain God's way of salvation. They bring the longed-for benefits of salvation with the Spirit who gives life. The law, on the contrary, has been proved by experience to be " the law of sin and death " (Rom. 8:2). It also lacks the power to produce righteousness. For if man is to become just before God, God must create him anew and impart new life to him.

22But scripture has made everything prisoner under sin, so that the promise should be given to believers through faith in Jesus Christ.

The law could not bring righteousness. On the contrary, the time of the law is characterized by the fact that everything was imprisoned under sin.. All men were under the rule of sin, and they could not gain their freedom through the law.

Scripture is here described as the cause of this state of things, because scripture proclaims and gives effect to the will of God. It does not merely declare that everything is held captive by the power of sin. The declaration brings about the imprisonment at the same time. For the word of God is not an empty echo of reality; it creates the facts of history.

God's will thus accomplished in scripture has a very definite object. The promises are to reach believers. At the present moment, the time of fulfillment, it is clear that God had this goal in view at the time when he was giving the law. What God promised is the heritage (3:18), which we are now receiving as the gift of the Spirit through faith (3:14).

It is the believer, therefore, who enters upon the heritage of Abraham. God gives the promised inheritance in such a way that it comes from faith in Jesus Christ. Faith in Jesus Christ is, therefore, not just the manner and the way in which the promised benefits are obtained. It is the source from which the inheritance comes down to us from God. The blessing of faith is now present. With the faith of the individual the conditions have been created in which God bestows on him the riches of the promise.

Paul now goes on to give a positive answer to the question about the purpose of the law. Negatively, he had said that it could not bring the life expected of it, and that it could not lead to righteousness. Positively, it was the role of the law to have been our tutor until Christ came (3:23-25).

²³*Until the coming of faith, we were closely guarded under the law, kept prisoners until the revelation of the faith that was to come.*

The decisive event in the history of salvation is the coming of faith. It came with Christ into the world in the form of faith in Jesus Christ. Abraham had no doubt believed, but he was only one individual: the age of faith begins with Christ. What went before was the age of the law. Paul knows, of course, that the promise preceded the law, and that it continued during the age of the law. But now he considers the decisive turning point, and so the period before the law was given recedes into the background.

The law had kept us all, both Jews and gentiles, under close guard, in prison as it were, or under severe control. We all had to experience the power of sin, and likewise death. For " sin lends arms to death, and the law lends force to sin " (1 Cor. 15:56). Man was a helpless captive within the mortal grip of the law.

Liberation took place through the revelation of faith. Faith as the way of salvation had long been in God's plan. Its revelation was already signaled as a future event while the time of the law was still in force. It was to be manifested by God as a heavenly mystery. And thus faith is seen to be a ray of the divine glory, which God will disclose fully to us at the end of time (Rom. 8:18). In Jesus Christ this glory has already become visible to us in faith. The dark days of imprisonment are over. Freedom came through faith, which God revealed. Freedom came from God.

24Thus the law was made our tutor till Christ, so that we might be justified by faith. 25But since faith came, we are no longer under a tutor.

With the word " thus " Paul draws the conclusion which results from the foregoing with regard to the role of the law. The coming of faith coincides with the coming of Christ. " Until Christ " the law performed its task of warder; it was, as it were, the custodian for our imprisonment.

But the phrase " tutor till Christ " has a deeper sense. The " tutor " (*paidagogos*) in the Graeco-Roman world was the unfeeling slave whose duty it was to look after the conduct and the welfare of the boys in a family, usually by scolding and punishing them. His activity was not that of a teacher. And the boys were

only in the charge of this supervisor from the age of about six to
sixteen. The " tutor " was usually not respected and never loved.
He treated the children harshly and corrected them severely,
while the reprimands which the father gave were quite different.
The law was this type of tutor. It was not an " educator " which
led up to Christ, but a harsh and heavy-handed supervisor from
whose charge we have been withdrawn since Christ came.

What then was the function of the law? It was not to be a sort
of gradual preparation for faith, to help us to win this way of
righteousness by our prayers. On the contrary, the law had a hidden meaning known only to God. It brought on sin.

But since faith has come, we are no longer under this tutor.
The law indeed persists in the world. But we free children of
God are no longer at its mercy; its power is broken (3:26).
Christ means " the end of the law " in the sense that the law is
deprived of its power. The believer has escaped its surveillance.
He attains righteousness as a free man.

To Belong to Christ by Baptism is to be a Descendant of Abraham and hence Heir of the Promise (3:26–29)

Since the coming of faith we are no longer under the tutor. Being
" sons of God," we are free from the law. We have put on Christ in
Baptism and so are " one person in Christ " (3:26-28). But whoever
" belongs to Christ " in this way is seed of Abraham as scripture
understands it (3:26). He is also the inheritor of the promise (3:29).

[26]*For you are all sons of God through faith in Christ Jesus.*

Paul addresses the Galatians personally once more. He reminds
them that they are " sons of God." This they are through faith.

For since its coming they are no longer at the mercy of the tutor. This is not the logical development of the idea of the tutor watching over the sons. For it was precisely the sons who were looked after by the slaves, till the day came for them to be removed from his charge. All Paul means is that the era when the law was in charge is now at an end. Supervision by slaves had the effect of turning their charges themselves into slaves, as it were. But through faith we have been set free. We appear before God not as slaves but as children before their father.

For we are now " in Christ Jesus." With these words, Paul describes the state of the baptized Christian, the relationship of the baptized to his Lord. The baptized is incorporated into Christ. As the next verse says, " he is baptized into Christ," he has " put on Christ." When the heavenly Father looks on the baptized, he recognizes in him Christ his Son. " If anyone is in Christ, he is a new creation " (2 Cor. 5:17). Baptism is the origin of a new life.

²⁷For you who have been baptized into Christ have put on Christ. ²⁸There is no such thing as Jew or Greek, there is no such thing as slave or free man, there is no such thing as male and female. For you are all one person in Christ Jesus.

Paul departs only ostensibly from the basic line of thought which he is pursuing. He shows apropos of baptism that this sacrament unites men so closely to Christ that one can really say that they are " in Christ Jesus " (3:26), that they are " one person in Christ Jesus " (3:28). But if the baptized " belong to Christ " so closely, then what is true of Christ is also true of them. They are seed of Abraham. They inherit the promise which was made to Abraham and his descendants.

The baptized are " baptized into Christ." In baptism one is " immersed in Christ." The immersion of baptism is an efficacious sign of being buried along with Christ (see Rom. 6 : 4). The baptized is indeed also crucified along with Christ (2 : 19). The death of the old man makes the resurrection of the new one possible. When man abandons his earlier being, he receives existence " in Christ."

All the baptized had " put on Christ " through being baptized into Christ. The new metaphor is that of being clad with a garment which enables one to play another's role. Christians have put on their Lord in this way. They have disrobed themselves of the old man and have clad themselves in the new. When Christ is their garment, then it can be said once more that they are " in Christ." They can say of themselves : " It is no longer I who live, it is Christ who lives in me " (2 : 20). They have a new being; they share in the being of Christ; they are a new creation.

It follows from this sacramental reality that all the baptized are " one person in Christ Jesus." This means that they belong to Christ so closely that they form one way of being with him (3 : 29). They are members of Christ, and what happened to Christ is verified in them. They likewise gain the promised inheritance, which was promised to Christ as the seed of Abraham.

This union with Christ is the basis of the abolition of the distinctions which made such a decisive difference in the ancient world—even with regard to the possibility of men's salvation. The religious distinctions of former times are eliminated. It no longer matters whether the baptized is a Jew or a gentile; his social standing no longer counts. Women too have access to salvation and to the promised inheritance. All distinctions have been wiped out by the waters of baptism; they are things of the past once Christ has been put on as a garment. The Christian is a new man in Christ. The new humanity formed by the baptized is no longer rent by divisions. It is thus seen by God and by the eyes of faith. In the eyes of the " old world," of course, the differences that have been secretly abolished still seem to be important.

29But if you belong to Christ, you are therefore descendants of Abraham and heirs by virtue of the promise.

The baptized belong to Christ not merely by their profession of faith and their following of Christ but in his very being. The Spirit of Christ, whom we received in baptism, made it possible for us to be united most intimately to Christ, to belong to him. For the Spirit of God is the Spirit of Christ.

The Apostle's argument has reached its goal. When scripture allotted the promises to the unique seed of Abraham (3:16) it meant Christ. But whoever belongs to Christ is incorporated in him, the seed of Abraham, and is himself seed of Abraham. If so, the promised inheritance also belongs to him, the whole blessing bestowed by God in Jesus Christ.

But the inheritance is attained by virtue of the promise. Paul emphasizes this once more at the end of the section to impress upon them the fact that the law is not the way to righteousness. The heir to the promise is united to Christ. To belong to him is to be " co-heir with Christ " and to partake of his glorification.

Christ Ransomed the Heirs. Thus They are Given the Position of Children of God (4:1–20)

The mention of the " heirs to the promise " leads Paul to take up another image. Having compared the promise to a testament (3:15-18) and the law to a tutor (3 : 19-25), he now chooses the metaphor of the heir who is a minor. Until he has reached his majority, the heir is like a slave. But he will certainly be of age some day. Applied to mankind, this means that with the coming of Christ the Son of God, we were freed from the law and became adult sons of God. The time of slavery and tutelage is over (4 : 1-7). If so, how can Christians wish to serve as slaves once more? Paul again addresses the Galatians personally. There should be no more turning back for them (4 : 8-11). Finally, he turns to his children with fatherly love. He begs them to listen to their father as they had done in the past (4 : 12-20).

On the surface, verses 1-20 do not constitute a proof from scripture. This is resumed only in 4 : 21f. But the passage is to be read in the light of the previous proof. They show how anxious the Apostle is to bring home to the Galatians the importance of the proof from scripture at the present juncture.

THE POSITION OF THE HEIRS BEFORE CHRIST WAS SENT: MINORS IN SLAVERY (4:1-3)

[1]Further, as long as the heir is a minor, he is no different from a slave, though he is the owner of everything, [2]but he is subject to guardians and stewards till he reaches the age fixed by his father.

Having shown in the previous verse (3 : 29) that those who belong to Christ receive the inheritance, Paul now strives to show what the inheritance means for them.

The image which he uses is taken from civil law, though definite parallels cannot be found for the individual traits. However, we have to remember that Paul heightens the imagery in view of the reality it illustrates. The metaphor presupposes an heir whose father is dead. This is not said in so many words, because this element of the metaphor cannot be verified in the reality to which it is applied. What the Apostle is interested in is primarily the minority of the child, which turns his existence into a sort of slavery. The other important point is that this period of the child's minority ceases at the date fixed by his father, when the child is installed as complete master of the estate.

A third point seems to be particularly emphasized in the metaphor. The Apostle says that the child, who has not yet obtained his full rights over the estate, is still the owner or lord of the whole inheritance. This points primarily to the fact that the child, though a minor, has full ownership of the estate. But when we envisage the reality depicted in the metaphor, it becomes clear that the guardians and stewards mean " the natural forces of the world " (see 4:3). These have reduced man to a slavery which is contrary to the will of the Creator. For when God made man, he made him lord of the world and of all things in the world (Gen. 1:28). As the Psalmist says: " You make him [man] lord over the works of your hands, you have put everything beneath his feet " (Ps. 8:7). The forces and the laws of nature do not exist to reduce men to slavery. Even the sabbath exists for the sake of man, as Jesus says (Mk. 2:27).

³So we too, when we were minors, were enslaved to the elemental spirits of the world.

The imagery, already heightened as we have noted in view of the term of the comparison, is now applied to those who are the heirs to the promise. The " we " of the statement includes Paul as well as the Galatians, Jewish as well as gentile Christians. In view of his gentile Christian readers in Galatia, the Apostle calls particular attention to the masters who once held them enslaved: the natural elements or forces. However, as a Jewish Christian, he could just as well have mentioned the law which had once been his guardian. The powers of nature likewise subject man to the service of their law (see 4:9f.). And on the other hand, the Jew's service of the law was also service of " this evil world " from which Christ has " rescued " us (1:4).

What is meant by " the elements of the world," as the Greek text runs, which we have rendered by " powers of nature " or " elemental spirits "? The Greek " *stoicheia tou kosmou* " means first of all the elements of which the world is composed, but must here mean the " elemental spirits " which, according to the beliefs of certain pagan circles, embodied the basic forces of the world, especially the stars. They are in fact compared here to personal beings, to guardians and stewards (4:2) who imposed their yoke of slavery on the Galatians before the time of Christ. They demanded the observance " of days, new moons, feast days and years." The Galatians worshipped them as gods, " which they were not in reality " (4:8). On the contrary, they are " weak and miserable " (4:9). They are utterly futile, as the gods of the heathen always are in the biblical view. Yet men tried to reassure themselves by placing their lives in the service of such gods. The conduct of the gentiles is therefore just as much in the service of law as the Jewish way of life which sought righteousness by efforts to accomplish the law. Jews and gentiles alike are subject to the law, slaves and minors till the " fullness of time " (4:4f.).

CHRIST RANSOMED THE HEIRS (4:4–5)

⁴But when the fullness of time came, God sent his Son, born of a woman, subject to the law . . .

The time of this world, the time of man's minority which was a sort of slavery, was of limited duration. The " fullness of time " had to come. Now the time of the Messiah has begun which brings men freedom from the law and installs them in their position as children of God.

At the date which he had set, " God sent his Son." The moment which brought this age to an end, according to God's will, also saw the coming of the Son. The messianic age and world replaces this age and the present world. God brings on " the world to come " by sending his Son. The literal sense of the Greek text is that God " sent out " his Son. The Son was therefore with God, and had divine being before his mission. He was sent into the world as the fully authorized envoy of God.

He was " born of a woman." He did not simply appear upon earth, manifest like a heavenly vision. He actually became man. St. John expresses it even more trenchantly in order to exclude any attempt to spiritualize the human reality of Christ: " The Word became flesh " (Jn. 1 : 14). Paul describes the incarnation as birth from a woman. In doing so, he does not intend to emphasize primarily the fact that Jesus became man by the action of the Spirit of God in the virgin Mary, but to bring out the " lowliness " and " humanity " of the man Jesus. This Jesus became one with us in the solidarity of human nature in order to free us. " Though he was rich, he became poor for your sakes in order that you should be enriched by his poverty " (2 Cor. 8 : 9).

The Son of God became " subject to the law." He not only shared man's human nature, he also shared his historical lot. He was placed under the law which enslaved all men. Though Son of God, he became by his mission a subject of the law. The emancipation of the slaves was to be rendered possible by the fact that the Son of God became like them, except in sin.

[5]*. . . that he might ransom those who were subject to the law, so that we might be given the position of sons.*

The goal of the mission of the Son of God in full solidarity with man is to ransom men from the law and, ultimately, to install them as sons of God. The work of the Son, therefore, is one of liberation. All men had indeed been enslaved, as it were, by " guardians and stewards," like the Jews under the law of Moses. God ransomed them. They are free.

There is still more. Through Christ's being sent by God, they were to be adopted by God as his children. Man the pauper was to be adopted by God the infinitely rich. To be adopted by a rich man in this way was regarded as a highly desirable honor in antiquity; how much more then to be given the status of child by God!

The train of thought, in keeping with 4:1-3, should really have led up to man's attaining his " majority." But Paul is thinking of the real state of things, which does not coincide at all points with the metaphor of the heir during his minority. For we are not children of God by nature, like *the* Son of God. On the contrary, we are granted sonship by a free and gracious act of God's will. It is to his grace alone that we owe our position as children of God.

THE SONS OF GOD RECEIVED THE SPIRIT (4:6–7)

[6]*But because you are sons, God has sent into our hearts the Spirit of his Son, crying " Abba, Father!"*

Paul once more addresses the readers of the letter personally, having already used " we " when speaking of Christians, meaning the Galatians and himself. The " you " of the plural in the direct address of 4:6 becomes the even more intimate " you " of the singular in 4:7.

The adoption of men as children of God is the reason why God imparted the Spirit of his Son. The dawn of the last times did not merely bring the advent of the Son of God into the world. It also brought the benefits of the promise to those who are through faith the children of God (3:26). They have received the eschatological gift of the Spirit. And thus the blessing of Abraham reached even the gentiles (3:14).

God sent the Spirit of his Son into our hearts. We have not then just attained the status of children of God. We are penetrated by the Spirit of Jesus Christ to the very depths of our being, in our very hearts. And his Spirit is the " Spirit of sonship " (Rom. 8:14f.). He gives us the proper attitude of the son towards the father, that of obedience in faith. This Spirit comes to the aid of our weakness (Rom. 8:26). He transforms our inmost being, giving man a new heart and a new spirit. When Paul recalls this new being, it is also meant to be an urgent appeal to all readers to develop the mentality of sons in the obedience of faith.

The Spirit himself cries to the Father: " Abba, Father!" He has grasped us so strongly that it is no longer we ourselves in person who pray to the Father, but the Spirit of the Son of God. Later, Paul will say that we cry " in " this Spirit " Abba, Father!" (Rom. 8:15). He is the divine creative power itself which enables us to cry out in childlike prayer.

Paul still makes use of the Aramaic form in addressing the Father, the form that Jesus had employed when speaking to his Father (Mk. 14:36). It is an intimate form of address, corresponding more or less to the familiar forms of the word " father " which children use today. It was precisely the way that a child spoke to its father. No Jew would have dared to address God in this way. But the Christian, being a child of God, may actually dare to address God as his father without more ado. In doing so, he does not forget that God our Father is in heaven (Mt. 6:9).

⁷So you are no longer a slave but a son, and if a son, then also heir, so made by God.

The cry of " Father!" uttered by the Spirit of God dwelling in our hearts makes it clear that we are no longer slaves but sons. For the Spirit bears witness " that we are children of God " (Rom. 8:16). Paul brings this home to every individual by using the second person singular here. In the sonship of each individual God's work of sending his Son has finally reached its goal. Through the coming of Christ, all have received the basic possibility of being transferred into the situation of children of God (4:4f.). Through the coming of the Spirit of Christ into the hearts of the faithful who have been " baptized into Christ," the true children of God (see 3:26-28), the individual becomes conscious of his sonship of God. It is now his task to live up to what he is and to show himself a child of God in his actual life: " For all who allow themselves to be led by the Spirit of God are children of God " (Rom. 8:14). The child surrenders himself in faith to the guidance of the Father; he looks to God in the spirit of sonship and not in servile fear.

To be son also means to be heir. The believer who has become son of God through Christ and his Spirit also inherits the promise. He is no longer a slave but the son entitled to his heritage. He is no longer a minor in the charge of a guardian, since the time has come for him to enter upon his inheritance.

The inheritance comes solely through God, through his gracious condescension; it is not achieved by any human act or effort. We are assured of the inheritance " in Christ." " If we are children, then we are heirs: heirs of God and co-heirs with Christ, if we suffer with him, to be also glorified with him " (Rom. 8 : 17). At the end of time God will reveal the glory of his children to all the world.

Do Not Relapse into Slavery! (4:8–11)

⁸Once, when you were ignorant of God, you were enslaved in the service of beings who in reality were not gods.

At one time in their heathen past the Galatians did not know God as he really was. They served gods who enforced demands on them, or rather, who were served by them in the hope of gaining security by a life of service. They lived and served as slaves.

They served beings who were not really even what they pretended to be and what they were supposed to be. The gods are in reality nothing of the sort. Paul is still thinking of the forces of nature, the elemental spirits of the world to whom the gentiles offered divine homage. It is in fact, according to the mind of the Apostle, the basic error of the gentiles that they " gave up the truth about God for a lie, and adored and revered the creatures instead of the Creator " (Rom. 1 : 25). Anyone who fails to recognize the Creator and his divine, creative omnipotence, must finally live in fear of the mighty forces that rule the universe, the violent upheavals of natural phenomena, and a destiny supposedly blind. He becomes a slave of nature and so a slave of its law. He is always anxious to conform to its laws to avoid the anger of the gods.

⁹*But now that you do know God, or rather, now that you have been acknowledged by him, how can you turn back again to the weak and miserable elements and offer to be their slaves once more?*

The " once " of ignorance is contrasted with the " now " of faith. Since faith came into the world, since the Galatians put their faith in God through the preaching of the Apostle, the darkness of ignorance has vanished and slavery under the powers of nature has been abolished. The Galatians have learned to know God; they know him now. When the mind has once recognized a truth, it cannot but know that truth. But it can ignore it and disregard it in practice. And for the Galatians that would mean a relapse into the former state of slavery. But surely, as the Apostle urges in his question, they are not going to do anything of the sort, against their own better judgment. After all, they have experienced in their own person the great change from their former slavery to their present freedom as children of God. Paul at once corrects the idea that knowledge of God can have its origin in man. Knowledge of God is not something that man can achieve. We have been known and acknowledged by him. Without God, who chose the believing Galatians and made himself known to them in the apostolic preaching, the change-over to the freedom of the children of God could not have come about. This reminder is perhaps more apt to preserve the former heathens from relapsing than their joy in the new knowledge of God. The certainty that God has known, chosen, and loved us is what constitutes the security of the believer in contrast to the existential anxiety of the pagan.

The Christian who has once known God cannot possibly return to the weak and miserable elemental spirits of nature.

Knowing that he has been acknowledged by God, he cannot wish to escape and take refuge with the powers of nature. The forces of nature may be impressive and powerful, but compared with God they are weak and miserable. They cannot provide the aid which one expects of them.

To serve the powers of nature once more would be nothing but slavery. Who could be so foolish as to want to exchange his election and his adoption as a son of God for the service of a slave? The new state of slavery would be even worse than the old. For the slave who was once a son can remember the time of his sonship only with sorrow and bitterness.

[10]*You note religiously certain days and the new moons and festive seasons and years.*

Relapse into slavery would mean that one would be slavishly anxious and painfully conscientious in trying to meet with the demands of the powers of nature. Paul now singles out the demands which paganism knew in common with Judaism. He could take this line because the Jewish-Christian innovators called on the Galatians to perform such works of the Jewish law as the exact observance of feast days with which observation of the heavenly bodies necessarily went hand in hand. On this point Judaism was in partial agreement with the religions of paganism. Paul can brand the efforts demanded by the Jewish-Christian zealots as relapse into the pagan worship of nature because both ways are equally erroneous. Both assert that human achievements in response to " divine demands " are necessary for salvation. The heathen way is a way of the law just as much as the Jewish. The religious attitudes and practices of heathenism prove to be slavish service under a law. But this very fact proves that the

Jewish way of law is fundamentally a pagan worship of nature. Who would wish to exchange the freedom which we possess in faith for such slavery? The believer is wholly dedicated to the service of God at all times, and not merely on certain sacred days.

¹¹You make me afraid that I have labored in vain among you.

Paul cannot repress the anxious cry: " Was everything I did use-less?" The fears of the Apostle should be a warning to the Galatians. They were no doubt astonished to hear that his missionary efforts could have been wasted. They undoubtedly felt that they could attain a more perfect stage of Christianity by following Paul's opponents. But no, they are not making progress in Christianity when they observe the law. They are falling away from God, who called them to grace (1:6).

The Apostle has fears for the churches, not for himself. If the Galatians yield to the demands of the agitators, they will fall from the state of grace and rush headlong to destruction. They should think of the unselfish and laborious efforts which the Apostle had expended on them. That too will help to avert the threatened apostasy.

LISTEN—AS BEFORE—TO THE APOSTLE! (4:12–20)

¹²Become like me! For I too became one of you. Brethren, I be-seech you! You have done me no wrong.

As the Apostle recalls the days when he himself worked among them, his appeal becomes more personal. Paul beseeches the Galatians, for they are and remain his brothers. They must not abandon the fellowship of brothers. The brotherhood that they once shared in common can provide stay and support for the individual.

Paul has not to shrink from presenting himself as an example. "Become like me!" For he has given up the performance of the law, which was the way he followed when he was a zealous Pharisee. The Galatians are perfectly well aware of that. The way of the law-abiding zealot is not the way of Jesus Christ. The Apostle continues to give the same example as the Lord. That is why he can write to the Corinthians: "Follow my example, as I follow that of Christ!" (1 Cor. 11 : 1).

The Galatians ought to be all the readier to imitate the Apostle because he too became one of them and lived like one of them. To those who were outside the law he showed himself as one who had disavowed the law; to the weak he showed himself weak. He became all things to all men in order to save all men (see 1 Cor. 9 : 21f.). This was not a calculated measure of adaptation. It was the fruit of a deliberate decision. He had abandoned the Jewish way of the law, and became thereby an apostate in the eyes of the Jews, no better indeed than a pagan.

Paul says all this to show how profound and brotherly is their fellowship. It has never been clouded by any personal injury done by the Galatians to the Apostle. They have not done him any wrong. They have not offended him personally. And so Paul does not wish to appear as the victim of insult. His reprimands are not stimulated by resentment or any secret grudge. They are called for by the situation. It is not the Apostle that the Galatians offend against when they give ear to false teachers but the gospel of God.

¹³*You remember how it was on account of an illness that I*

preached to you at first, ¹⁴and though my bodily state was repellent to you, you did not treat me with contempt or horror, but you received me as an angel of God, as Jesus Christ.

To show the Galatians that they have given him no offense, Paul reminds them of the warm relationship by which they were once united to him. He recalls the time when he first preached the gospel to them. The memory should prevent their committing an injustice now. They must now bring clearly to mind something that they could easily have forgotten in the course of time: the joy with which they had received the good news of the gospel. How easily the Christian grows accustomed to the joyousness of Jesus' message, and how readily he takes it as a matter of course!

It was on account of an illness that he had stayed with the Galatians for the first time. He had not planned to make a stop in the " land of the Galatians " on his second missionary journey (Acts 16:6). When his illness forced him to rest, he made use of his stay to preach the gospel. Though the illness was a temptation for the heathen Galatians, they had not succumbed to it. For heathen listeners, a message stands or falls with the impressiveness of the preacher's figure, and with the enthusiastic vigor with which it is delivered. But Paul was neither impressive nor vigorous. And so his outward bearing (his " flesh " in the Greek) constituted a serious temptation for his hearers. Still, they did not despise him. They did not regard him as a sick man possessed by demons, the sort of person whom they usually regarded with horror and spat out against. Sick man though he was, they recognized in him the messenger of salvation and hence of joy. They received him as an angel of God, not as the carrier of demonic powers. They succeeded in overcoming their pagan prejudices.

Indeed, they recognized in him the Apostle of the Lord himself. They gave him a welcome as though he were Jesus Christ. For he who receives the envoy of the Lord receives the Lord himself (Mt. 10:40). Anyone who has grasped even the elements of the good news will not find the sickness and infirmity of the preacher a stumbling block. Such a messenger can often be a more tangible proof of the presence of the Lord, who took upon himself our weaknesses.

[15]*What has become of your blessedness? For I can assure you that you would have torn out your eyes and given them to me, if that were possible.* [16]*Have I then become your enemy by telling you the truth?* [17]*They are eager to win you, though to no good purpose. For they want to shut you out, so that you may be eager for them.*

Paul asks reproachfully what is left of their former happy enthusiasm. When they first became Christians, they were so full of joy that they would have done anything for the Apostle of Christ. They would have given him the most precious part of their body, their very eyes. What has become of the glad generosity of those days?

The coolness that has displaced the former bliss gives rise to the suspicion that the Galatians now regard Paul as their enemy. Did Paul make himself their enemy by proclaiming the truth, by putting before them the gospel which freed them from the law, fully and clearly and truthfully?

No, that cannot be the reason. The intruders with their false doctrines are canvassing vigorously for the support of the communities. And the Galatians know that these men are to blame. Hence Paul does not have to mention their names. But their zeal is not zeal for the good. On the contrary, it comes from their jealousy. They themselves wish to be eagerly sought after in their role of "Super-Christians" who go so far as to observe the Jewish law.

Their intention in all this is to shut out the Galatians. They are jealous enough to want the whole attention of the Galatians. They want to separate the communities from their teacher Paul, and to exclude them from grace (1 : 6f.) so that they may finally claim the Galatians as their own followers (see 6 : 13). The aim of the true preacher of Christ, however, is not to assure his personal standing by the number of his followers, but to minister to the salvation of his hearers in Christ the Lord: "For we do not preach ourselves, but Jesus Christ as Lord, and ourselves as your servants for the sake of Jesus" (2 Cor. 4 : 5).

¹⁸*It is well to be urged to do good at all times, and not just when I am with you,* ¹⁹*my children, with whom I am once more in travail, till Christ is formed among you.* ²⁰*I wish I were with you now, and could speak in a new language, for I do not know how to approach you.*

It is well to be won for the good, and that is what Paul wants. He allows himself to be canvassed by the emancipated, and he wishes to be sought after on the same terms by the Galatians. When he was with them, they carried him shoulder-high, so to speak. They should still be his zealous partisans when he is no longer with them. Their loyalty should persist unchanged even when Paul is far away.

For the Galatians are still Paul's children. That is how the Apostle addresses them now as he pleads with them so urgently and paternally. Indeed, his love is the pain-racked love of a mother who is in the throes of childbirth.

Christ is to take form among them. That is the object of the new birth pangs which Paul is suffering for the sake of his communities. The travail consists of preaching anew the truth of the gospel. The process of birth must be repeated to a certain extent, since the Galatians are on the point of falling away from grace and separating from Christ (5:4). When they received baptism they put on Christ (3:27). They became one person in Christ (3:28). So Christ must now be embodied among them; the communities should be visible to the world as the body of Christ. That is the ultimate goal of Paul's preaching. To attain this goal, the Apostle suffers pains like a mother. No matter how painful he finds it, he tells them the truth.

If Paul could now be in Galatia, his personal appearance would assure his success. If he could in fact speak a new language, speak with the tongue of angels (see 1 Cor. 13:1), the Galatians would be bound to listen. But Paul, some hundreds of miles away, cannot do this. He has now used every possible tone of human speech in his letter, from curt severity to pressing exhortation and motherly love. What approach can he now use? What is he to do to win them back?

Pay Heed to the Teaching of the Law Itself: You Are not Children of the Slave but of the Free Woman (4:21–31)

Completely at a loss, Paul argues once more from the word of God. Thinking things over again, he has come upon a supplementary proof, again from the story of Abraham. The law itself gives testimony to the provisional character of the law. What Paul now proposes for consideration is found in the law, that is, in the five books of Moses which were accepted as divine teaching (Torah). To inherit the promise it is not enough, as the Jews think (see Mt. 3:9), to be a child of Abraham. One must be a child of Abraham like Isaac, not like Ishmael. It must be " by virtue of the promise," and not through descent " according to the flesh " (4:23). True sonship of Abraham does not come from being born " according to the flesh " but through descent from Abraham " according to the Spirit " (4:29). Christians are " children of the promise like Isaac " (4:28). This is the main line of thought to which others are annexed. Ishmael, the son of the slave is contrasted with Isaac, the son of the free woman, Sarah (4:22). And as Ishmael in his day persecuted the son of the free woman, so too today the true, free, children of Abraham are persecuted by those who are children only according to the flesh (4:29-30).

The Two Sons of Abraham (4:21-23)

²¹You are anxious to be subject to law. Tell me then, do you not hear what the law says? ²²It is written in the law that Abraham had two sons, one by the slave and one by the free woman. ²³But the son of the slave was born according to the flesh, while the son of the free woman was born by virtue of the promise.

Paul now asks the Galatians for an answer, as if he were in their presence. Their readiness to yield to the Apostle's opponents shows that they are anxious to place themselves under the law (4:9). Their choice of way to the heritage of Abraham, therefore, would be the law. But the point is that this is impossible for any-one who listens properly to what the law, the heart of the Jewish scriptures, has to say.

Paul sums up the account given in Genesis of the patriarch's sons (16:15; 21:1-21) and shows that scripture speaks of two sons of Abraham whose parentage is very different. One of them, Ishmael, is the son of the maidservant Hagar, the slave whom the patriarch had taken as his concubine. The second is Isaac, the son of the free-born lady, Sarah.

But there is another great difference apart from their mothers. They differ radically in the manner of their birth and their subsequent lives. Ishmael saw the light of day by the ordinary process of procreation, while Isaac was born by virtue of the promise. He owes his existence not merely to the natural way of conception, but also to the divine promise.

HAGAR BORE CHILDREN TO SLAVERY (4:24-25)

²⁴All this has a hidden meaning. The women represent two testaments, one of them, Hagar, that of Sinai, which bore children into slavery. ²⁵For the word Hagar signifies Mount Sinai in Arabia. She corresponds to the Jerusalem of today, for Jerusalem and its children live in slavery.

Paul comes to the application of what scripture meant by the two different women and their sons. The Apostle finds a significance which goes beyond the historical persons in question. Scripture speaks to him in a way which suggests hidden meanings: it is an " allegory " which means something more than it says and points to a hidden meaning.

Thus the two women who occur in the history of the ancient covenant become types of new realities in the new covenant. They point symbolically to two rival testaments. They are figures which stand for two different dispensations of divine providence. One of the women, the first to give birth, is the covenant of Mount Sinai, which is the " ancient covenant " from the standpoint of the new.

This woman, representing the covenant of Sinai, an essential element of which is the law, bears children into slavery. The slave Hagar cannot give free men to the world. So too the testament which she stands for cannot bring forth children that are free. Anyone who is bound by that covenant lives the life of a servant and a slave.

Paul now undertakes to show why Hagar means the covenant of Sinai. The name Hagar is probably of Arabic origin. And Hagar was looked on as the ancestor of the Ishmaelites, who lived as nomads and peddlers in northern Arabia and the steppes east of Jordan. Thus from every point of view Hagar indicates Arabia, which is the country of Mount Sinai.

But the testament of Sinai, the ancient covenant, is in force to-day—at the time of Paul—in Jerusalem. The Jewish religion involves its followers in the slavery of the law of Sinai. The bondswoman Hagar who bore children into slavery belongs essentially to the Jerusalem of the present day. She corresponds exactly to it, since Jerusalem too lives in a state of slavery along with its children.

We Are Children of the Free Woman (4:26–31)

26But the Jerusalem on high is free and she is our mother.

Without developing fully the comparison with Sarah, Paul now goes straight to the point of his argument: the free woman is our mother. Paul omits the consideration that Sarah, whose name means "princess," represents the divine arrangement whereby children are born into freedom, and that she stands for the new covenant which took its start from Christ and the coming of faith. This new covenant of freedom is not to be found in an earthly city.

Its situation is the Jerusalem on high. It must have been a scandal to Jewish hearers when the holy city with the temple of God was compared to the outcast Hagar. But Judaism also was familiar with the idea of a heavenly Jerusalem, which is contrasted with the Jerusalem of this world. The Jerusalem on high is in the heavenly world of God. If then we are children of this city, if we are citizens of it (Phil. 3:20), we no longer belong to the world's ancient age but to the new creation which God has inaugurated. To this heavenly Jerusalem we Christians owe our life and our way of life, which is freedom. The new world is already present in the church, and so as children of the free woman we must live our lives in freedom from the law.

²⁷For it is written:

" Rejoice, O barren woman, you childless one,
Burst forth in cries of joy, you who have not been in travail;
For the lonely woman has children,
many more than the wedded one " (Is. 54:1).

We could already sense the jubilation of the Apostle in verse 26 when he spoke of " our mother," but now the quotation from Isaiah shows unmistakably the full extent of Paul's joy. The prophet spoke in the days of Israel's exile of God's new covenant of grace, and now his words are being fulfilled. The barren woman must cry aloud for joy because she is blessed with countless children.

How can the prophet's words be applied to the Jerusalem on high, to the free-born Sarah? For Paul understands them as a proof of the new freedom of Christians (4:26). The Book of

Isaiah speaks figuratively of Sion or Jerusalem as a woman (for example, 49 : 14-21). At the time of the Babylonian captivity Sion is, as it were, lonely and abandoned by her husband. Sion can no longer look forward to the blessing of children. The people seems doomed to extinction. At this moment of solitude and desolation, the prophet pronounces his jubilant prophecy of God's return to Sion, his " spouse." Jerusalem will once more be blessed with children. Sarah too was barren and despised. But God intervened miraculously and she became the ancestor of a mighty people. Hence the oracle about Jerusalem which reminds the hearers of Sarah is an excellent indication of what God means to do at a later time. The prophecy that Sarah or the Jerusalem on high will be blessed with numerous children has now been fulfilled. The Galatians have the joy of sharing directly in the great miracle of the divine fulfillment. Will it prevent them from doing what they have in mind?

²⁸*But you, brethren, are children of the promise like Isaac.*

This is the end of Paul's proof from scripture. The main line of thought was only interrupted by the cry of jubilation. If the Jerusalem on high, the free-born woman, is our mother, then the Galatians (whom Paul now addresses directly once more) are children of the promise like Isaac. They will no longer desire the existence of slaves, such as is represented by Hagar and her son.

²⁹*But just as once the son born according to the flesh persecuted the son born according to the spirit, so too at the present day.* ³⁰*But what does scripture say? " Drive out the slave and her son. For the son of the slave shall not share the inheritance with the son of the free woman "* (Gen. 21 : 10).

Though the proof is finished, Paul makes another point which is in the nature of an answer to an objection. He speaks of the persecution of Isaac by Ishmael, who, according to Jewish understanding of the allusion in Gen. 21 : 9, gave free play to his moods with regard to the son of the free woman Sarah. The son born " according to the flesh " was a rival who laid traps for his brother who was born " according to the spirit."

Instead of speaking of Isaac as the child born " by virtue of the promise," Paul now chooses the expression " according to the Spirit." He is already thinking of the application of the event of former times. Through the Spirit of God, Christians are children of God and of the heavenly Jerusalem. What took place between Ishmael and Isaac is being continued in the days of the Apostle. The children of the earthly Jerusalem, the thralls of the service of the law, are persecuting the children of the Jerusalem on high, the church. They may appear to be more powerful than the children of the free woman, which is a temptation for the Galatians. But in reality the persecution proves that the children who are free are the heirs to the promise.

Scripture puts this beyond doubt. It cannot be the will of God that there be two heirs, because only one of them can enter upon the inheritance. Sarah's order for the expulsion of the slave corresponds to the will of God (Gen. 21 : 12). Legalistic Judaism cannot inherit what God has promised. And that must be the fate of everybody who has received his life " according to the flesh " or who leads such a life. It must be noted that the call to expel the slave is not directed to the Galatians. They are not asked to expel the persecutors of the church of God because the call is not addressed to the Galatians. And the summons is not meant for them indirectly. For even within the quotation it is not addressed to Sarah or Isaac, who prefigure symbolically the children who are free. However, the Galatians may feel confident in spite of the persecution of the church by the synagogue. The will of God has allotted the inheritance to the persecuted.

[31]Thus, brethren, we are not children of the slave but of the free woman.

This is the second and last postscript to Paul's proof from scripture. He appeals once more to the bond of union which joins the Galatians and himself. Speaking in the first person plural, he addresses them as his brothers. If they remember the " spiritual " nature of their origin, they will want to lead their new life likewise " according to the Spirit." They will not want to base their lives on the flesh.

We are not children of a bondswoman or slave. As Christians, we are the children of the free-born woman. That is the conclusion which results from the allegory of Sarah and Hagar. Since the traits of Isaac, when interpreted allegorically, are verified in Christians, these are the true children of Abraham, the heirs of the promise, the children of the free woman. They have a new existence " by virtue of the promise " in the power of the Spirit of God. They are, therefore, free from the burden of the law.

CHRISTIAN FREEDOM
AND LIFE IN THE SPIRIT (5:1—6:10)

Having proved from Christian experience and from sacred scripture in the second part of the epistle that righteousness does not come from the works of the law but from faith, Paul goes on in the third part to apply the truths thus acquired to the life of the communities. To this extent, one may contrast this ethical part of the work with the two previous parts, which were autobiographical and apologetical (part I) and doctrinal (part II). In the view of the Apostle, however, ethics does not simply coincide with exhortations and directives. Christian ethics is based on the nature of Christian being. That is why Paul had to lay such a broad and deep foundation before he could erect upon it the building of Christian conduct.

But even this part of the letter which contains practical rules of conduct continues the demonstration of how what *we ought* to do grows out of what *we are*. It begins with an appeal which forms a resumé of the letter, and takes up the theme suggested by the last scripture proof—"freedom in the Spirit or slavery under the law" (5:1-12). Those who are called to freedom must not, however, confuse freedom with libertinism. On the contrary, Christ sets us free for love of our neighbor (5:13-15). This love with all its manifestations is again the fruit of the Spirit (5:25—6:6). The last section shows that true Christian perfection does not grow out of the ground of the flesh. The eternal life of the baptized is the harvest of what man has sown on the ground of the Spirit, that is, on the ground which God himself has prepared through Christ (6:7-10).

Christ Set us Free, not for a New Slavery but for Freedom (5:1–12)

The Yoke of Slavery (5:1–3)

¹*Christ set us free to live in freedom. Stand firm, then, and do not let the yoke of slavery be imposed on you once more.*

Freedom is the keynote of the Christian life. This was the last word and the end result of the scripture proof in 4:21-31. Paul uses the same word to begin the new section of the letter. Christ has emancipated us to be free men. He has not, for instance, just rid us of the burden of slavery for a moment; he has placed us permanently in the state of free men. That is the status which we now possess in Christ (2:4).

Christ has set us free to be free men, to enjoy the condition into which we have been transferred by his redemptive death on the cross, and now we live in freedom—we have been assigned to this state. It is freedom from the law, a freedom which the Galatians would renounce if they adopted circumcision (5:3). But since Paul here uses " freedom " in a comprehensive sense, the word also includes freedom from sin. For where the law holds sway, sin is developed and strengthened through the law. The law " gives sin its force " (1 Cor. 15:26). To escape the law is to be outside the clutches of sin. The Christian liberated by Christ is also set free from death, of which sin is the cause (Rom. 5:21) and also the sting (1 Cor. 15:56).

He who enjoys such freedom through Christ must stand firm in it, and surely will. He will be determined to preserve his status of free man. He will keep his dignity in mind.

But he who allows himself to be enslaved will find that he

totters under the weight of the yoke. He will groan under the slavery of the law, because the burden will be too much for him. For the Galatians it would mean a relapse into the legalism under which they once lived (4:9). They must not return there again.

²Listen to me. I, Paul, tell you that if you are circumcised, Christ will be of no use to you. ³And I affirm once more that everyone who lets himself be circumcised is obliged to keep the whole law.

Paul now interposes his whole apostolic authority to tell the Galatians what it actually means if they undertake to be circumcised. The " Listen!" underlines the decisive importance of what is coming. " I, Paul, tell you " implies the apostolic responsibility as well as the authority of the envoy of Christ, who once also expected righteousness from the law.

Whoever is circumcised will find Christ " of no use." If the Galatians choose circumcision as the way of salvation, they are very much mistaken. They will not advance in Christianity to a higher level of perfection: all they do is to ensure that the salvific work of Christ will be wasted as far as they are concerned. The Galatians have not yet taken the decisive step. If they decide in favor of circumcision, Christ will not declare that they are righteous when he passes judgment on them.

Why will Christ be of no avail to the gentile Christians who let themselves be circumcised? Paul assures everyone who is circumcised, that is, every gentile Christian who takes the way of legal righteousness by being circumcised, that he is obliged to keep the whole law. Circumcision launches the Jews on a way of life based on the law, where they seek to attain righteousness by accomplishing the law (5:4). Anyone who adopts circumcision submits himself to the antiquated and obsolete order of the law, and must keep the law in terms of all its precepts. He must keep the whole law.

Paul's opponents have undoubtedly not disclosed this to the Galatians. They have not described the law as a yoke, but have only spoken of circumcision as the way to true sonship of Abraham and to the heritage of the messianic age. Paul, however, shows the Galatians that the law is a yoke (see 4:9f.), and its claims must be fulfilled to the last detail (3:10). The false teachers themselves, who praise the law as the way to righteousness, in their quality of Jewish Christians do not comply with its all-embracing demands.

Faith Active through Love (5:4-6)

⁴If you try to be justified by the law, you are cut off from Christ, you have fallen from grace. ⁵We, however, await in the Spirit our hoped-for righteousness, by means of faith.

The Christian who adopts the way of legal righteousness by being circumcised is not only bereft of Christ's aid and delivered over to the curse of the law, he is also cut off from Christ. The bond that united him to Christ is dissolved; he is eliminated from Christ " in whom " he existed through baptism (3:27f.). But the word which Paul uses for being " cut off " from Christ also has the meaning of being destroyed and annihilated. Thus anyone who tries to be justified by the law has set the seal on his own destruction.

He has " fallen from grace." For he falls away from God who

has called him to grace (1 : 6). The Christian under the gospel is
in the realm of divine grace, and anyone who betakes himself to
a pseudo-gospel falls away from grace. Through faith man has
access to grace, and through baptism he is in the state of grace.
Who would wish to leave the realm of the blessing for that of
the curse?

How then do we Christians await righteousness? The first
point to note is that we do await it. It comes as a gift from God,
not as an achievement accomplished by our own powers. It is a
blessing that we hope for. Even the baptized and believing
Christian has not yet reached the point where righteousness is
decisive. The last judgment has not yet come, and final perfection is not yet there. But the baptized is not simply in a state of
waiting, faced with uncertainties. He has a well-founded hope. If
he perseveres in grace, if he is steadfast in the freedom given him
through Christ, God will perfect him in righteousness. Christian
fulfillment is not attained by our pressing onwards. It is bestowed
at the end by the action of God. But we must persist in the freedom of the gospel and in grace.

We start on the way to righteousness by means of faith. We
follow it in the Spirit. Thus Christian life and Christian ethics
mean a way of life that is guided by faith. And faith becomes
effective through love. The moral life of the baptized is faith in
action. It is also life in the Spirit. For the Spirit of God is the
force that impels us along the way of life which leads to
righteousness.

*⁶For in Christ Jesus neither circumcision nor the lack of it means
anything: all that counts is faith, active through love.*

Paul once more gives the reason for what he said. He discloses the reason why we Christians rightly expect righteousness from faith, and why those who wish to be justified through the law have fallen from grace. In Christ Jesus there is only one power which can effect righteousness, and that is faith. In the new order of salvation which has dawned with Christ, the difference between being circumcised and not being circumcised has lost all meaning for man's salvation. The distinction which formed an unbridgeable contrast within the realm of the law is no longer valid in Christ.

What is valid is faith active through love. The Christian too, for whom faith is the force that brings about righteousness and salvation, has an activity. Faith becomes active in love. And so faith and love go together in one who is baptized in Christ. Faith cannot exist without the love which makes it active and gives it real effect. And love too without faith is impossible, because faith is the source from which the new life of the baptized draws strength. Such faith has the power to make men righteous.

The Following of the Truth (5 :7–12)

⁷You were running well. Who hindered you from following the truth? ⁸Whatever arguments were used, they did not come from him who calls you.

His description of Christian existence is a painful reminder to the Apostle that the Galatians " ran well " till the Judaizers arrived. They had striven hard to translate their faith into action through love.

It is astonishing that their course has been held up. It is hard to conceive how it could have happened. But happen it did, and they are being hindered from following the truth. They are ready to abandon the truth of the gospel. They are ready to play false to what they are in Christ. But there can be no good reason for what they have in mind.

Their first fine efforts have been paralyzed by persuasive arguments. But such arguments cannot echo the will of God. God's call today must be in harmony with what they heard when they were first called. The call to be circumcised and hence to keep the law does not come from God. The messengers who urge such things on the Galatians cannot be from God. But the true Apostle, Paul, summons his communities to return to the truth of the gospel as he had preached it to them from the start.

⁹A little yeast will leaven all the dough. ¹⁰For my part, I have confidence in you, in the Lord, and I am sure that you will not change your minds. But whoever is disturbing you will feel the weight of God's judgment, no matter who he is.

The comparison with the working of yeast expresses an everyday experience. In the case of the Galatians, it is a reminder that even a few agitators can succeed in infecting the whole mass of the Galatian communities. They can easily succeed in imposing their demands on the Christians, especially as these Christians hope to find a higher form of Christianity in the law. This is the process which must be checked.

The Apostle affirms, however, that he has confidence in them, in the Lord. He relies on the fact that they will agree with him. They will now see the truth of the gospel more clearly and stand by it, like Paul. An expression of confidence, when pronounced by a father to his children, can be more effective than a mere warning or threat. And when this confidence is based on the

Lord, he will help these wayward children to escape the danger and he will maintain them in the truth.

Whoever causes disturbance in the Christian communities will have to bear the weight of God's judgment and punishment. For God cannot but pronounce sentence of doom upon anyone who approaches the churches of God with a message opposed to the gospel of God. And their punishment is all the surer because these disturbers of the peace call their message another gospel, that is, a message from God.

No matter who they are, such preachers will not escape punishment. Presumably there must have been one or other distinguished personage among the agitators. But the Apostle does not mention any of his opponents by name. He probably felt that this would have been to do them too much honor.

11But if I, brethren, am still preaching circumcision, why am I still being persecuted? If that was so, the scandal of the cross would be eliminated.

Paul now attacks a false and pernicious picture of his preaching, such as has perhaps been popularized by his adversaries in order to cause confusion. On the one hand, they have challenged the real message of Paul with the argument that Paul is not a true Apostle of Jesus Christ (see 1 : 11f.). On the other hand, they seem to have been saying that Paul himself still advocates circumcision —still " preaches circumcision." They claim that Paul has remained basically what he always was, a Jew, who even as a Christian expects righteousness to come by way of the law, and hence through circumcision. Paul gives two proofs to show that this cannot have been implied in the Pauline preaching.

He is still being persecuted. He has had enemies plotting

against him ever since he ceased to advocate circumcision, ever since he was called to be an Apostle (2:4). This is still true at the present moment, as the activity of his opponents in Galatia demonstrates. If these adversaries were right, the scandal of the cross would be eliminated. For while his adversaries urge circumcision, Paul proclaims Christ as the crucified, which is a scandal for the Jews (1 Cor. 1:23). They take offense at this because the cross is for them the shameful gibbet which they abhor. And so they reject the scandal which confronts them in the cross. They persecute Paul because his whole preaching is centered on the message of the cross (6:14). The persistence of the scandal of the cross proves that the Apostle has never ceased to preach the crucified and not circumcision (6:12).

The cross is for Paul the new sign of salvation now that circumcision has been abolished. It is the one exclusive means of attaining righteousness. While circumcision is the essential emblem of the accomplishment of the law which is supposed to lead to salvation, the cross sums up and signals the grace which rejects the observance of the law and acquired privileges. That is why the Apostle takes no pride in " the flesh " of his followers, but only in " the cross of our Lord Jesus Christ " (6:13f.).

[12]*What a pity that these trouble-makers do not have a complete excision performed on them!*

The section closes with a sarcastic wish. It is that the trouble-makers who are shattering the brotherly unity of the churches would take the drastic measure of having themselves castrated. Then they would have still more reason for fleshly boasting on their own principles. In their pious efforts to achieve something, they would be going still further than those who " only " have themselves circumcised. But then—a point which will certainly not escape these former Jews—they would be excluding themselves from the community of God (see Deut. 23:2).

The general tendencies of Paul's opponents are here associated once more with paganism. For the mystery cult which had its main center in the Galatian city of Pessinus featured the self-castration of the priests of Attis and Cybele as a religious rite. When Paul now associates circumcision with this pagan horror, he is not merely making a bitter jest which must sound blasphemous to Jewish ears, he is demonstrating the profound agreement between one who seeks salvation by the Jewish way of the law and the pagan who tries to win the favor of the gods by extraordinary achievements. Basically, they both have taken the same wrong turn.

The Most Important Principle:
To Serve One Another through Love (5:13–15)

Paul has firmly rejected any compromise between law and faith (5:1-12). This is again explained by recalling the freedom (5:13a) which has been bestowed on the Galatians. What is demanded of the Galatians will now come up in some detail, but first the Apostle enunciates the fundamental law of all Christian ethics, which is love (5:13b-15). Love of the neighbor should fill up, as it were, the space newly gained by freedom.

¹³For you have been called to freedom, brethren.

Christians are called to freedom. The Apostle addresses his readers once more as brothers. The freedom which Christ introduced in principle by the redemptive act which threw open the

possibility of freedom to all men became a reality among the
Galatians when God called them. At the moment when God
called them through Paul, the Galatians, as people of God, as
the church, were called out of the old world of men and placed
in freedom. They were rescued from the present evil world (1:4)
and placed in the new creation of God (6:15). But the call to
freedom still continues to have effect. The emancipated must
take the side of freedom and stand by it.

[13b]*Only do not let freedom be a springboard for the flesh, but
serve one another through love.*

Anywhere that freedom is preached, it can be wrongly understood. There will always be people who take freedom to be the
arbitrary wilfullness of egoism. Paul is aware of this: freedom
can become " a springboard for the flesh." It can be abused by
selfish men to give free play to their lower nature. They can
easily feel themselves to be lordly creatures in their new-found
freedom. And then in the " fleshly " way of the children of this
world they try to evade the service of God. What they want to
do takes the place of what they ought to do, and they attack
each other like wild beasts, ready to bite or devour each other
(5:15).

The danger of such abuse of freedom among the Galatians
seems to have been not very far away. Paul is certainly not giving
warnings against a theoretical possibility. And it may very well
be that the Apostle is here addressing the same men whom he
warned earlier against relapsing into the slavery of the law (5:1).
The spiritual blindness which results from " performances " in
legal terms often finds reasons for evading the tasks of everyday
life. The vanity of the " idealistic " innovators, who are so full

of their self-importance, could easily start a fashion among the Galatians (5:26). This leads inevitably to mutual rivalries and jealousy. It turns the friendly unity of the churches into a war where everyone's hand is against his fellow.

"Serve one another through love." Brotherly service of one another is the way of life which corresponds to freedom in Christ. To be free in Christ is to be free "for love," because love occupies, as it were, the space made by freedom. It is likewise freedom "of love," because love alone gives men freedom to do "what they wish." Love is the "law" of the Christian. It is not law in the sense of detailed norms and precepts, but in the sense of being the foundation of all Christian action.

This service of love is the Christian's way of being a slave. He does not serve the flesh, but he is a slave to the service of his neighbor. In such slavery he not only preserves his status of free man. Love in the form of service is the full realization of freedom in Christ. Christ's service and sacrifice are the model for this service of our brethren.

14For the whole law is fulfilled by one commandment: "Love your neighbor as yourself" (Lev. 19:18).

It may sound contradictory, but it holds good for the Christian: when freedom is understood as being set free for love, then in such freedom—which is also freedom from the law—the whole law is fulfilled. Paul quotes a commandment which had by no means a prominent place in the "law" and received no particular emphasis in the ethic of the Old Testament. It referred to love of one's fellow countrymen. But in Jesus' eyes, the commandment calls for a love great enough to embrace all mankind. Further, he provides the commandment of charity with its profoundest reason: he founds it on the basic commandment of total love of God, as in the Old Testament (Deut. 6:5). Love of God and love of the neighbor are, as it were, the two aspects of the one and the same principle on which Jesus focussed all morality. No " greater commandment " exists (Mk. 12:28-34). This explains why love must even extend to enemies (Mt. 5:43-48); the true child of the heavenly Father loves all men in God for the sake of God's love. Paul is following whole-heartedly the teaching of Jesus when he says that to keep the one commandment of love is to fulfill the whole law.

What does the commandment of love imply more exactly? It is significant that he does not mention what regards God directly, the exigencies of the love of God. " Love your neighbor!" That is what matters to him here. Love of God can be easily spiritualized in such a way that love of the neighbor is overlooked. But anyone who thinks that he is loving God while he is disregarding his fellow men, his neighbors, his companions, is deceiving himself. For the one two-fold commandment of love is indivisible. " If anyone says, I love God, and still hates his brother, he is a liar " (1 Jn. 4:20). Love must prove itself in the service of the needy whom we meet. What love of the neighbor involves can be explained by love of self. Everyone loves himself naturally, aims at his own welfare, and wishes good to himself at all times. That is the way we must be intent on the welfare of those who are close to us, of those who cross our path, of those whom Christ sends to our door. We must love them as we love our own self. Christ demands of all who belong to him that they love their neighbor as themselves. In the Sermon on the Mount, the principle of charity is illustrated as follows: " Whatever you would wish men to do to you, do you also to them " (Mt. 7:12a). That is more than the negative way of understanding freedom which is contained in the proverb, " Do nothing to anybody that you would not like done to you "—which is merely an effort to secure the individual against aggression.

¹⁵*But if you continue to bite and devour each other, you will bring each other down to destruction.*

The " if " with which Paul starts his sentence does not merely consider a possible case. It refers to what is actually happening among the Galatians. They are attacking each other like wild beasts that bite and devour each other. The movements which are gaining strength in the communities are leading in fact to personal enmities and jealousy: jealousy about the accomplishment of the law, where everyone tries to outdo the other, and jealousy about possession of the Spirit, badly misunderstood, which ends up in inconsiderateness and vanity (6:1).

Paul warns his readers with bitter irony of the only possible outcome of this law of the jungle. It means that the churches which the Apostle has built up will end by destroying themselves. The Christian communities will disappear in an orgy of mutual destruction. That is what zeal for the law leads to. But a grateful regard towards grace, as experience also shows, leads to brotherly love and a flourishing community life.

Love is the First Fruit of the Spirit (5:16-24)

Paul now shows how it is possible to stand fast in the freedom of love. He speaks of " life in the Spirit," that is, of a life lived under the direction and the impulse of the Spirit of God, the promised blessing bestowed on all Christians (5:16). But when Christians endowed with the Spirit still experience " the desires of the flesh "

(5 : 16-18), this struggle need not leave them without consolation. For as men who belong to Christ, " they have crucified the flesh with its passions and desires " (5 : 24).

Paul uses this line of thought as a sort of framework into which he inserts a catalogue of vices and a catalogue of virtues (5 : 19-23). These two lists describe the armies, so to speak, which are opposed to each other in the battle of life. On one side is the defeated army of the " works of the flesh." Here the Apostle is not enumerating vices which he seriously thinks occur in practice among the Galatians. But he holds them up as a warning to them, to show them where zeal for the law may again lead them. It bars the way to the heritage of the kingdom of God.

On the other side is the " fruit of the Spirit," where Paul places love first of all. But the fruit of the Spirit, the gift which he can bring, is manifold. Against such gifts, there is no law; where the Spirit rules, there is freedom, and the power of the law is at an end.

The Desires of the Flesh Are Against the Spirit (5 :16–18)

[16]*But I tell you: walk in the Spirit, and you will not fulfill the desires of the flesh.*

Paul now goes on to explain the line of thought which he indicated above. He had exhorted his readers not to make freedom an excuse for following their lower nature. He had urged them to serve one another through love. He had warned them against mutual provocation in the communities. Now he makes his point clear by using a concept of which the communities had a vivid memory. He says: " Walk in the Spirit." The Galatians received as Christians the Spirit of God. They set out on the Christian way of life in this Spirit. Are they now to end in the flesh? They have experienced the action of the Spirit of God in the life of the community. Now they too must walk in the Spirit, follow the path, and lead their lives in the strength of this Spirit. Their life must correspond to what they really are. They must walk with their eyes fixed on the Spirit who is their rule of life. They will do this if they allow themselves to be led by the Spirit. To make use of one's freedom for love means, therefore, to allow oneself to be led by the Holy Spirit. The Christian does this by listening obediently to the Spirit.

If so, he will not fulfill the desires of the flesh. It is impossible for a Christian who lives his life in the Spirit to connive at the desires of the flesh. Paul can be confident of this because the two powers, the Spirit and the flesh, pursue radically different ends. Hence the Spirit, who is in truth the Spirit of God, can thwart the power of the flesh. Just as it is impossible to understand " Spirit " here as the spirit of man, so too " flesh " (*sarx*) cannot be understood simply as " our flesh." The Apostle takes *sarx* here as a personal power which encompasses us and towers above us. It has its desires by means of which it summons us to nullify our own real will. But where it finds itself opposed to the Spirit of God in us we shall not fulfill its desires.

[17]For the flesh has desires contrary to the Spirit, and the Spirit has desires contrary to the flesh. For these are opposed to one another, so that you do not do what you will.

The struggle between Spirit and flesh is not to be understood as the rivalry between the higher spiritual self and the body of man. On the contrary, the whole Christian man is the theater of the battle between Spirit and flesh. The power of the flesh is directed against the presence of Christ in us. The hostility of the flesh to Christ is expressed in the " desires of the flesh." But the Spirit too has desires, contrary to the power which tries to bend man to its will. Both powers have their own desires.

We are not to do what we wish. The flesh tries to repress all action which comes from a will such as is found in one who is led by the Spirit. And the will of the Spirit is to hinder any fleshly action which man might wish to perform by consenting to the desires of the flesh.

18But if you are led by the Spirit, you are no longer under the law.

It is all-important, therefore, that the Christian allow himself to be led by the Spirit, that he fall in with the intentions of the Spirit of God, that he let himself be guided by the Spirit of Christ. Following this divine guidance, he will fulfill the law by a life of love. Thus he lives in the freedom to which he is called without setting up " his own righteousness " (Phil. 3 : 9).

He is really free because he is no longer under the law. The Spirit masters the fleshly strivings of man which urge him either to a self-conscious pride in his achievements under the law, or to act contrary to the law.

The Works of the Flesh (5 :19–21)

19aThe works of the flesh are unmistakable . . .

The inexorable struggle between flesh and Spirit is not confined to the human heart, where the conflicting desires of the two powers are experienced. The opposition between the two leaders becomes clearly visible as soon as the ends pursued by them are envisaged. These ends are manifest wherever the respective desires have been realized in human action. When Paul now lists the various vices one by one for the Galatians, he is evoking realities which can arouse salutary fears in Christians. He is not primarily concerned with urging them simply to avoid this or that particular vice. He is showing where the desires of the flesh will lead if one gives way to them. The fifteen vices which Paul enumerates are summed up in advance by the words " the works of the flesh." He uses the plural " works," in contrast to the singular of the " fruit of the Spirit " (5:22), because he wants to indicate that the deeds of the flesh are of all sorts, a confused multitude, a mass of inextricable disorder. Paul follows no fixed order in listing the vices; some are in the singular, others in the plural. These are the chaotic conditions which the flesh produces, in contrast to the Spirit.

The expression " works " also suggests something else. Paul gives the title of " fruit " to what the Spirit produces in man, but what the flesh produces are called " works." The flesh performs deeds which man can claim as his own achievements, but which end up in the confusion of vice because they are fleshly achievements. The Spirit, however, produces " fruit." The activity of man under the impulse of the Spirit leads him to give thanks to God for the gifts he has received. The Christian acts by virtue of the divine Spirit, and so his action culminates in a marvelous harmony of the gifts of the Spirit, all blended in charity. God the creator forms a moral world of order and peace.

[19b]*They are fornication, unchastity, licentiousness,* [20]*idolatry, witchcraft, enmities, quarrels, jealousies, anger, strife, divisions, factions,* [21a]*envy, drunkenness, orgies, and the like.*

The first three examples of the works of the flesh consist of sexual disorders: fornication, unchastity, licentiousness. Fornication means sexual intercourse outside marriage. The second word refers to the moral " impurity " which can result from sexual misconduct; it is a more comprehensive word, because it includes the impure intention. The third word indicates unbridled sensual excesses, which are accompanied often enough by sexual license.

Sexual disorders are not the only manifestations of the desires of the flesh: a wrong type of divine worship also follows. This too is a typical pagan fault. The fault of the pagan consisted in the fact that they " exchanged the majesty of the eternal God for the image of a mortal man or a bird, beast or serpent " (Rom. 1:23). The pagan tries to get control of the divine in his idolatrous worship; there too, according to Paul, the desire of the flesh shows itself. Witchcraft stems from the same root. Heathen magic ascribes divine power to objects and actions which cannot have such properties. By learning to handle these things, it believes that it can control the action of God.

Now come the vices, in no particular order, which menace social life. They are sins which grow out of selfishness in men who know nobody but themselves. Personal expressions of hostility lead to quarrels or result from quarrels. The enmities of the quarrelsome often stem from jealousy. " You are still fleshly," writes Paul to the community of Corinth, " for where jealousy and quarrelsomeness reign among you, are you not fleshly and are you not behaving according to your lower nature?" (1 Cor. 3:3). Outbursts of anger and strife are concrete manifestations of enmity. Rising anger always vents itself in outbursts of rage, and enmity is always given to intriguing with kindred souls. Thus personal enmities lead to divisions and factions. The works of the flesh end by splitting up the community to further group interests. They turn the divine order of things into a jumble of ruins.

With the last three vices, which have to do with licentiousness, Paul takes up once more the cruder aberrations. Envy (or more exactly, various forms and expressions of envy, since the word is given in the plural) leads up to the sins which occur at parties: drunkenness and extravagant orgies of all kinds. The catalog of vices ends with the conventional phrase " and the like," which means that the list of sins could be prolonged almost indefinitely. The works of the flesh are as prolific as they are destructive.

²¹ᵇAnd I give you notice, as I gave you before, that the people who do such things shall not inherit the kingdom of God.

The Apostle now calls attention to the inevitable consequences of a life according to the flesh in the hope of deterring the Galatians from doing the works of the flesh. The object of enumerating them was that they could see what must happen if a Christian abandons himself once more to the desires of the flesh. Anyone who does so will not inherit the kingdom of God. The works of the flesh exclude one from the kingdom of God. He who performs them will not be an heir to the fullness of salvation at the coming of Christ, since Christ does not save him from the wrath of judgment.

Paul gives the Christians of Galatia advance warning of this. But he had already foretold it on an earlier occasion when speaking to them as pagans. The announcement of judgment is also part of the gospel message, precisely when addressed to pagans. The Apostle repeats it to the Christians as a warning to them. Just as it is true that they have already attained righteousness through faith in Jesus Christ, so it is also true that they will finally be judged according to their works. There their state of righteousness will be decisive for final salvation or loss.

The kingdom of God, like righteousness, is not attained by our achievements. They are inherited by the children of God. They are a gift of God's fatherly goodness. Just as when Jesus speaks of the " kingdom " or " lordship of God " the exercise of God's power is always implied, so too when Paul speaks of the righteousness or justice of God he always supposes the judgment of God on mankind. Though the kingdom of God and the righteousness of God come to us as gifts, they also come as tasks to be fulfilled.

The Fruit of the Spirit (5:22–24)

²²*But the fruit of the Spirit is love, joy, peace, patience, friendliness, kindness, loyalty,* ²³ᵃ*gentleness and self-control.*

The opposition between the works of the flesh and the fruit of the Spirit, is called upon to keep to this Spirit, to direct himself the multiple and the one. The orderliness of the moral world, created by the Spirit of God, is reflected in the triple rhythm of the well-balanced enumeration. The fruit of the Spirit consists of three times three virtues. Their unity is indicated by the fact that the Apostle speaks of " fruit " in the singular and not of " fruits." The moral life of the Christian is in fact one single thing since it is service through love. It is in love of the neighbor that the work of the Spirit begins and reaches maturity. While the extraordinary effects of the Spirit, the charismas, attest the work of the Spirit in the church (3:5), in the individual who possesses the Spirit through baptism, the fruit of the Spirit is manifested as love. For the love of God is poured out into our hearts in the Spirit. Faith becomes active in love. Being Christian love, it is of course first directed to God. But in our text Paul thinks of love of the neighbor, for it becomes visible as the fruit of the Spirit. Every work of the Christian, insofar as it is not a " fleshly " work, contains this love as fruit of the Spirit.

Joy is the next thing mentioned by the Apostle. It is the joy evoked and imparted by the Holy Spirit. Its ultimate foundation is the hope which comes from the good news of the gospel, the nearness of the Lord. It does not allow itself to be troubled by tribulation and distress because it is more than good spirits. In this it follows the example of the Lord and his Apostle.

Peace comes in the third place. The Spirit aims at the peace, the well-being of man, while the end and object of the flesh is death. Peace is one of the elements which constitute the kingdom of God, which " does not consist of eating and drinking, but of righteousness and peace and joy in the Holy Spirit " (Rom. 14:17). The peace to which God has called Christians, which he has established through Christ, can, as the " peace of God," " guard our hearts and our thoughts in Christ Jesus " (Phil. 4:7).

Patience, friendliness, and kindness are virtues which preserve joy and peace in human intercourse. The patient man puts up with others even though provoked enough to be angry. He remains unmoved, steadfast, and tolerant. He is magnanimous towards all. For the Christian, the necessity of magnanimous patience results from the example of God, who graciously restrains his just anger. Friendliness and kindness are positive efforts to help his fellow men. He serves them by his friendly presence and his responsive goodness.

Loyalty, gentleness, and self-control conclude the list, which of course makes no effort to be complete. Loyalty must be the basis of confidence among the community, just as treachery spreads the distrust which undermines the community. Gentleness implies meekness and modesty, the opposite of arrogance. Such gentleness is to be characteristic of those " endowed with the Spirit "; Christians do not reprimand each other in vengeful anger or with uncalled-for severity. The Christian has been given the example of gentleness by Christ. Last comes self-control, which is more than abstinence. It is undoubtedly placed here in opposition to the vices of sexual license and unbridled libertinism. Self-control is the fruit of the Spirit. But it cannot be maintained without constant struggle and exercise.

[23b]*Against such things there is no law.* [24]*But those who belong to Jesus Christ have crucified the flesh with its passions and desires.*

No law can be against such fruit of the Spirit. A life led in obedience to the Spirit fulfills the law (5:14) and therefore does not have the law against it. Where the Spirit holds sway, the power of the law has come to an end. In saying this, Paul underlines what he has already said: " If you are led by the Spirit you are no longer under the law " (5:18). And he who allows himself to be led by the Spirit of God is likewise no lawbreaker.

The decision in favor of the Spirit and against the flesh has already been taken in principle by Christians. They have opted against the flesh, and so they can begin a life in the Spirit. That happened at baptism, where they were incorporated sacramentally into Christ and clothed with him (3:27f.). And thus they belong to Christ (3:29). But what took place once for all in baptism must now be lived.

The baptized have crucified the flesh. They have slain it, as it were, so that it can no longer carry out its work of destruction on them. Earlier, the Apostle described this as the action of God himself on the baptized (2 : 19); here he says it is the action of man. He is thinking of the decision which the baptized person himself has taken and by which he must abide. By submitting himself to baptism, the believer crucified the flesh with its passions and desires—the flesh whose works have just been enumerated. He has delivered himself over to Christ Jesus and so to the Spirit; he belongs to the world of the new creation. " In Christ," he is " a new creation " (2 Cor. 5 : 17).

Life in the Spirit is Brotherly Service (5:25—6:6)

Though the Apostle has already said what was necessary when depicting the works of the flesh, and especially when disclosing the fruit of the Spirit, he goes on all the same to indicate some particulars. His aim is to show how life in the Spirit is to be lived.

Life in the Spirit (5 :25–26)

²⁵*If we live in the Spirit, let us also walk in the Spirit.*

We live in the Spirit. That is the starting point of our moral life. Our life comes from the power of the Spirit, the life that began for us in baptism. Christ lives in us (2 : 20). We are penetrated by the Spirit.

It follows that we must let ourselves be guided by the Spirit. We would not be living according to our inmost essence as Christians if we did not walk in the Spirit. Paul here uses a more precise word for walk than he did earlier (5 : 16). He spoke there of " walking around " in the Spirit, but here he uses a word which is a military term. Its original meaning is " to fall into line," " to march in regular order," " to direct oneself." The same word occurs later (6 : 16). There it has the definite sense of " holding to (a course, a norm)." The Christian, since he lives in the Spirit, is called upon to keep to this Spirit, to direct himself by this Spirit.

[26]*Let us not strive for empty honors, challenging one another, envying one another.*

Paul starts his precise admonitions considerately by saying: " Let us." He includes himself in the admonition. But he is also suggesting that the Galatians should be at one on this point with the Apostle, whose only boast is the cross of Christ. The troublemakers in Galatia, however, wish to boast and cut a fine figure (6 : 12f.). The Christian does not strive for empty honors. He means something in the eyes of God. He is also a respected brother to his brother. But he does not seek for vain, empty, illfounded honors. He has no futile urge for self-assertion which makes him want to be admired by his fellow men. He does not seek respect and honors like the fleshly man.

Anyone who does so, who is conceited in this way, challenges others. He provokes the same conceit in others. Each one then tries to outdo the other. The honors one seeks do not correspond to the honor that one has.

And finally, one is envious of the other. He begrudges the other the advantages which he has or seems to have. But " in the Spirit," each one leaves the other in possession of his standing, because he knows that what he possesses is the grace of God.

Bear One Another's Burdens (6 :1–6)

¹Brethren, if one of you is caught out in a fault, you who are endowed with the Spirit must correct the person in question in a spirit of mildness, while you, my friend, look to yourself, so that you may not be tempted yourself.

Paul now addresses his readers urgently as " brothers." He is coming to an important admonition which affects the recipients of his letter directly (" You must "). The reason for his directive, which is likewise the motive for carrying it out, is given in two stages : Christians are endowed with the Spirit, and each of them ("you, my friend ") is exposed to the temptation to sin.

Paul takes up an important matter in the life of the community. A member of the community is " caught out in a fault." Someone has discovered him committing it. No matter how grave the sin is, the other may not play the role of judge. He must show that he is obedient to the Spirit.

The term that Paul uses here may perhaps contain an ironic allusion to an honorable title, which the Galatians applied to themselves in a wrong sense. Then what he is saying to them is : Yes, you are really " endowed with the Spirit," but you must not pretend that you are superior types, dealing condescendingly with the unfortunate. The Spirit whom you possess demands gentleness when dealing with a brother.

Where the correction is not given in the spirit of mildness, it is a work of the flesh; outbursts of anger can only bring with them strife and enmities. But where it is given lovingly and gently, for the good of souls, it imitates the mildness with which Jesus met sinners.

The Christian who corrects his brother must also " look to

himself." If he thinks of his own case, he will not forget that everybody commits faults, because everybody can be tempted. Even the Christian endowed with the Spirit is treading a steep and narrow path, from which he can slip and fall. If a brother has fallen, he must try to set him on the path again. It is at the very moment when the Christian loses sight of his vulnerability that temptation is at its strongest. " Anyone who thinks that he is safe should make sure that he does not fall " (1 Cor. 10 : 12).

²Help each other to carry your burdens, and you will be fulfilling the law of Christ.

Christians help each other to carry their burdens. They are, of course, spared the burden of the yoke of the law. But Christian life too has its burdens which often weigh too heavily on the individual. The burdens in question are probably not just the loads imposed on us by our being open to temptation, but also those imposed by human weakness and malice. The presupposition of this mutual aid is that we do not " live to please ourselves " but " to please our neighbor in all that helps and strengthens him " (Rom. 15 : 1f.). This is the imitation of Christ.

By such mutual aid, the " law of Christ " is fulfilled. Paul coins a phrase here which is a challenge to the old law, whether Jewish or gentile. The new world which has arisen since the salvific death of Christ also has a law, namely, the law of Christ. Judaism also expected a new law from the Messiah. However, it was not to abolish the old law, but to give it a new and perfect interpretation. Christ, on the contrary, brought a completely new order of things; he is the end of the law (Rom. 10 : 4). This new order of things is based on faith and on faith's working through charity, and in the last resort on the activity of the Holy Spirit.

It is the Christian's way to righteousness. It is the way he inherits the kingdom of God. The Apostle can say to the Christian: " The law of the Spirit of life in Christ Jesus has released you from the law of sin and death " (Rom. 8:2). The law of Christ also makes demands. It demands brotherly love. But this is the fruit of the Spirit and hence leads to life. The demands of the old law, however, occasioned self-righteousness and so led to sin and death.

³For if anyone thinks he is somebody, he is deceiving himself, for he is really nothing.

Here too, as a little earlier (6;1), Paul bids his readers to consider their own case, to further the service of the neighbor. We have to help to carry one another's burdens, because each of us after all is " nothing." Anything that we are we have received. And what we have gained by our own efforts is in no way decisive in the eyes of God. It would be a baneful self-delusion to fancy ourselves in any way on account of our being Christians or on account of our supposed perfection, and worst of all, to compare ourselves with others.

⁴Let each one test his own performance, and then he can take pride in his own achievement and not by comparing the achievements of others.

Such illusions will be avoided if each one tests himself and hence his own performance. He will then cease to compare his work with what others have done or failed to do. He will measure it by what God demands of him. But can he then take pride in it? If he can, it is only because he knows that Christ is the only reason why he can boast, and the only thing he has to boast about. For the Spirit whom we possess " in Christ " has brought forth his fruit in us. All our good works are the gift of God.

⁵For each one will have his own burden to carry.

The saying about each one having to carry his own burden sounds like a proverb. It is inserted to give the reason why each man must examine his work. The Christian is bidden to do this because he himself is responsible for his work. He has to bring it to God for judgment. He will not be able to point to the advantages which he had compared to others. For he has nothing of his own to boast of. He cannot survive without the operation of the Spirit of God, who makes it possible for him to produce his own work. Everyone must take responsibility for his life's work, of which the gift of faith and the power of the Spirit form the foundation. He will have to bear it into the presence of the divine judge.

⁶Everyone who is being instructed in the faith must share all the good things which he has with his teacher.

Once more the Apostle exhorts Christians to make common cause with one another, and this time it is a matter of the fellowship which those who are receiving instruction (the catechumens) should maintain with regard to those who give instruction (the catechists). Paul is here thinking of the teachers who regularly undertake the task of giving Christian instruction in the communities. Perhaps the churches were at the stage when groups of disciples were being formed around various teachers, as we know existed in Judaism where the doctors of the law had their own personal disciples.

The pupil must share all good things with his teacher. Fellowship thus becomes dedication to one another's interests. The teacher imparts the benefits of the faith, the pupil gives in return the good things which the teacher needs for his maintenance. Paul takes it for granted elsewhere too that the preacher of the gospel will be furnished with earthly goods by the community. But here Paul is not speaking of what concerns the community as a whole. He is thinking of the personal obligations of each hearer of Christian doctrine. The Galatian Christians in particular, with their pride in possessing the Spirit, must have been tempted to overlook these simple matters of everyday life.

To Sow in the Spirit
is to Harvest Eternal Life (6:7–10)

Paul uses the image of sowing and harvesting. The confident expectations of the countryman are based on the fact that one reaps what one has sown. The harvest is reaped at the hour of God's judgment. This too is a Christian motive for moral action. God will repay at the end. He requites either with eternal life or eternal loss. But this retribution depends on whether one has decided in favor of the Spirit or the flesh.

⁷Make no mistake: God does not let himself be treated with contempt. A man will reap whatever he sows.

We are now at the last section of the exhortations, and Paul introduces this part of the letter with an appeal to his readers not to let themselves be deceived or mistaken. Anyone whose sense of possessing the Spirit leads him to think that " ordinary " and " everyday " trifles cannot be of decisive importance when seen against life as a whole is the victim of a grave illusion. Even these little things can lead to the loss of eternal life. They are not always very noticeable, but that is the very reason why they can be overlooked. The Christian must examine his conscience and test himself in these matters.

For God does not let himself be treated with contempt. God is in fact despised when someone takes pride in the possession of the Spirit bestowed on him by God, but does not direct his life according to this Spirit. But he who opposes the Spirit closes his heart to God. And God owes it to his divine majesty not to allow himself to be treated with contempt. He will requite such conduct on the part of man. He does not allow himself to be treated with derision, like someone who cannot defend himself.

To explain the decisive character of human action, Paul quotes a proverbial saying: " A man will reap whatever he sows." Man has a choice, and can decide on whatever seed he likes. And he determines the harvest when he chooses the seed. We must, of course, notice that Paul is not taking over an assertion of contemporary philosophy without more ado. In the next verse (6:8) he remolds the metaphor in a Christian sense. He felt that this philosophy basically made the harvest of human life depend entirely on the choice of the seed, that is, on human achievement in life.

For he who sows on the ground of his flesh will reap corruption from the flesh; but he who sows on the ground of the Spirit will reap from the Spirit eternal life.

The image of the reaping being determined by the sowing is changed somewhat when it is applied to the Christian life. It is not now the seed which is decisive, but the ground in which one sows. He who sows in his flesh will reap corruption. He who commits his fate to his own proper earthly existence, and hence expects fruit from the flesh and from fleshly action, can only reap corruption from the flesh. For only works of the flesh can grow out of the flesh. It can only give rise to vices which lead to destruction. The crop which is ripening now in secret will become manifest on the day of Jesus Christ. The harvest will then be brought in.

But the Christian who sows in the Spirit will reap eternal life from the Spirit. He who takes the Spirit as the ground of his actions, that is, he who allows his actions to be directed by the Holy Spirit, will reap the harvest of eternal life from this divine field. Hence eternal life is not simply the reward of our good deeds. It is not given to us because our deeds in themselves earned such a reward. The harvest of eternal life depends on the ground of the Spirit, who inspires our action till the harvest grows out of it. For the Spirit of God gives life and brings forth fruit.

[9]But let us never tire of doing good, for we shall reap the harvest in due course, if we do not grow slack.

To sow in the Spirit means to do good. Good deeds receive their good quality from the Spirit. They are done by us, but their source is the Spirit. They are accomplished by men but in view of the Spirit, since they are done according to the Spirit and his will. That is how man does what is good.

The Christian may easily find it exhausting to do what is good. But he may not tire. His life is in fact a race during which he may not stop and rest. And we must not allow ourselves to be disheartened by those who continue to pass a " fleshly " judgment on all human action, that is, evaluate everything by its outward success. The good that we do is done in the Spirit and therefore has an inward power of its own. Hence we can never grow lax. The harvest belongs only to the tireless.

I might very well wish at the present moment that the harvest time had already come, now that I have done good. But the harvest comes in due course, and only God knows when the time is ripe. In the meantime I must continue to live and act in the Spirit. " He who perseveres to the end will be saved " (Mt. 10 : 22). This is true above all under persecution by earthly powers and in the tribulation of the last days, in which " the charity of many grows cold " (Mt. 24 : 12f.).

¹⁰ *Well then, as long as we have time, let us do good to all, but especially to our fellows in the faith.*

At the end of his exhortations, Paul appeals to the Galatians to do good to all. No one is to be excluded from their charity. But since we cannot come in contact with all men, we must prove that our love is genuine in our own immediate circle. It must be exercised in the form of good deeds done to our fellows in the faith. For they are the people who live in the same house of God, the church, as we do. Each member of the " household of the faith " has been brought by God's grace into the same family of God as I myself. Each is my brother.

As long as we have time! With these words the Apostle presents the time to the harvest, the time when the seed is sown and grows, as our great opportunity. We still have the time and the chance to do good. We must make use of our time.

THE CLOSING OF THE LETTER
(6:11-18)

The Closing Written
in the Apostle's Own Hand (6:11)

11Notice the large letters in which I am now writing to you with my own hand.

Up to this point the Apostle had dictated the letter to a scribe, but now he writes with his own hand. It was not customary to sign one's name at the end of a letter in antiquity. The usual thing was to add some final remarks in one's own handwriting. Paul follows this custom.

He writes in particularly large letters. This is something which is attested in the time of Paul. The parts of a document which we would now underline or bring out by heavy print were then written in particularly large characters. Thus the Apostle intends to emphasize once more in conclusion the main interest of his letter. " Notice," he says in order to claim the whole attention of his readers once again. What he now writes merits to be underlined. Being written by the Apostle, it has an official character. Paul speaks to the Galatians by virtue of his apostolic authority.

The Unmasking of the False Teachers (6:12–13)

12All those who want to play an impressive role in the flesh are trying to force you to be circumcised, but only to escape being persecuted for the cross of Christ.

Paul finally disposes of his adversaries by disclosing their real nature and purposes to the Galatians. They are making deliberate efforts to have circumcision adopted among the Galatians, as the Christians know well. " They are trying to force you to be circumcised." The insistence of the trouble-makers comes very close to coercion. But their success is not yet assured.

Paul therefore exposes the secret motives of his opponents. " They wish to play an impressive role by means of the flesh." By practicing circumcision on the flesh of Christians, they hope to appear as successful preachers in the eyes of the world. They want to be able to boast of the flesh of the Galatians. But the very fact that they wish to present the flesh of the Galatians as their great triumph shows very clearly the " fleshly " character of the trouble-makers themselves. Their whole mentality is that of the older world which has been reduced to nothingness by the cross of Christ. Their efforts are not guided by the Spirit.

There is another motive too behind the efforts of Paul's adversaries, which also manifests a " fleshly," selfish attitude. They do not wish to be " persecuted for the cross of Christ." If they preach the whole message of the cross of Christ with all its consequences, they will be persecuted by the Jews. But if they preach circumcision as the way of salvation, the Jews will not mind even if they also speak of Christ incidentally; for they would then be no more than the heads of a special movement or sect inside Judaism. Hence the motive which impels the false teachers of Galatia is a very selfish one. Basically, it is a matter of cowardice. And with this they are poles apart from the Apostle, who preaches the cross courageously and rejects circumcision as the way of salvation, even though he suffers persecution for this very reason.

¹³*For even those who have themselves circumcised do not observe*

the law; but they want to have you circumcised so that they can boast of your flesh.

The Jewish-Christian agitators do not themselves observe the law. Either they are unequal to keeping it, or they do not want to. Here it is important for Paul that the very people who have been circumcised and who press for the circumcision of the Galatians do not themselves obey the precepts of the law. That is the contradiction in the Jewish way of salvation. One is bound by virtue of circumcision to observe the whole law; but it cannot be kept in full. However, the Apostle is hardly alluding to this contradiction here and to nothing else: he wishes to lay bare the profounder motive which is behind their effort. In the last resort, they are not really interested in the fulfillment of the law. What they really want is to be able to boast of the flesh of the Galatians. If they urge circumcision, it is not because they are zealous for obedience to the law. Their vanity is the driving force. Their proposal of circumcision for the Galatians is not made to satisfy the demands of the law, but to pander to their own ambitious pride. In this motive too they are the opposite of Paul.

Paul Boasts of the Cross of Christ (6:14–16)

[14]*But as for me, God forbid that I should boast, except of the cross of our Lord Jesus Christ, through which the world is crucified to me and I to the world.*

The Apostle flatly disowns all such pride in the flesh as his opponents seek. The words " God forbid " are at once a firm confession of faith and a prayer. The Apostle has understood the importance and significance of the death of Christ and is steadfast in his faith. He knows that there can be no more boasting on the basis of human achievement: he knows that the grace of God justifies through the cross.

In the view of Paul, if there is anything left to boast about, it is the cross of Christ. What his opponents think of as horrible and shameful is a matter of pride for Paul. And this boast does not result from his own glorious deeds; it comes through the divine act of redemption through Christ. And man becomes something to boast about, because he becomes righteous before God through the cross of Christ. But such praise, by reason of the cross, does not ultimately honor man but the cross, and hence God himself.

The sort of boasting which the old world of the law indulged in is rejected by Paul on the grounds of the basic fact recognized by faith: through the cross, the world is crucified to the Christian; and at the same time, the human ego is crucified to the world. The cross was the means whereby God crucified the world and the " old man." Through Christ's death on the cross, the world and its claims on man were given over to death. The world can no longer count on the lower nature of him who has in baptism " been crucified along with Christ " (2:19). This man no longer exists for the world. Through the cross of his Son, God has pronounced sentence of death on the old world of the law and sin, and also on the " old man " of self-seeking achievements in terms of the law. God has silenced the boasting of the world and of fleshly man, to make place for the praise of him to whom alone praise is due. Thus the cross of Christ is efficacious not merely with regard to the man who accepts it in faith as his way of salvation. It also has cosmic effects, since it makes the old world null and void, and opens up the way for the new creation.

[15]For circumcision is nothing, and uncircumcision is nothing; there is only a new creation.

The new world can be characterized negatively by saying that circumcision is nothing and uncircumcision is nothing. Through the cross of Christ, circumcision and uncircumcision have been deprived not only of their force but of their very existence. In the eyes of the world indeed they still exist, but for God and before God they bring about no essential mode of existence. They simply do not exist before God and with reference to salvation. The circumcised is not just before God, just as the uncircumcised is not thereby unjust.

The face of the cross turned towards us is the new creation, which became visible, along with the risen Lord, to his own. Christ is the first-born of those who slept. Those who were crucified with Christ in baptism were also raised up with him (Rom. 6:4f.). They are in Christ the men of this new creation: "If anyone is in Christ, he is a new creation. The old is past, the new has come" (2 Cor. 5:17). To be a man of the new creation therefore means to be "in Christ." And this again means in actual life faith and love. In Christ, however, the unity of mankind is restored on a higher level: Jew and gentile, circumcised and uncircumcised exist no more; there are only children of God.

Therefore, Paul can boast of the cross. The pride of the Christian also contains true joy and genuine self-respect. The Christian rejects the self-satisfaction of the children of the world. And his pride in the cross is ultimately praise of God. But he is glad to be a child of God in the new creation. He is really proud of belonging to the family of God in Christ. He is an enthusiastic member of the community which represents the new people of God, the church.

¹⁶*And all who direct their lives according to this rule: peace upon them and mercy, and upon the Israel of God!*

The Apostle now pronounces the blessing upon all who live by this rule. Though he is anxious to bestow the blessing of God upon all, he knows well that the Galatians are in danger of giving up the basic rule of the Christian life. Hence the word of blessing contains a hidden warning against putting oneself out of reach of the blessing. Since the new creation has dawned, the Christian must look to it in all things. He must guide himself by it. But if he considers the standards of the old, doomed world, if he thinks of circumcision as necessary for salvation, the blessing of God does not rest upon him.

Peace and mercy are showered down by God on those who are his true children in the new creation, on those who hope for their salvation from the grace of God. They will be granted what they hope to receive as a gift. They live at peace with God in the new world and in this peace all is well with them. They will experience God's mercy at judgment, for God has made them just. The will of our heavenly Father, which is to rescue us from the present evil world (1 : 4), reaches its goal in them.

When Paul was giving his admonitory blessing, he was thinking primarily of the Galatians, who he hopes will keep to the norm of the new creation. But he finally takes in all Christians. They are the new Israel of God. The church is the people of God in the new world created by the death of Christ on the cross. The promises of God are for them. They are now contrasted with the " Israel according to the flesh " (1 Cor. 10 : 18). It is their pride and their obligation to be the people whom God has chosen as his own.

Final Exhortation and Blessing (6:17–18)

[17]In future, let no one cause me trouble; for I bear the scars of Jesus on my body.

In a forceful conclusion, the Apostle demands that no one should cause him trouble in future. No one is to be burdensome to him again, neither his opponents with their plots nor the Galatians with their weakness. The curt summons expresses the wish and the firm expectation of Paul, who hopes to put an end to the whole affair with his apostolic letter. Hence he appeals to his apostolic authority to reinforce his demands.

For he bears the scars of Jesus on his body. The marks which his apostolic service of the Lord have left upon him make him resemble the Lord. And hence Paul's scars are the hallmark of Jesus in a two-fold sense. But there is a third allusion: the ancient reader would have been reminded by these words of the tattooed sign which brands the slave as the property of his master. And so it is clear that Paul thinks of himself as the slave of Christ (1 : 10) who is protected by the hallmark of his master. The Galatians will presumably be very careful not to resist the slave of Christ.

[18]The grace of our Lord Jesus Christ be with your spirit, brethren. Amen.

The last word to the Galatians is a word of blessing. It is as though the Apostle has already won back the Galatians. He does not send any personal greetings to individuals as in other letters. But he imparts to the communities the grace of our Lord Jesus

Christ. Though this form of blessing occurs in other letters also, it had a special overtone for the Galatian readers: the favor and the gracious providence of God come to them through Jesus Christ.

The last word before the " Amen " is the friendly title, " brothers," which does not occur in the final blessing in other letters of Paul. Writing to the Galatians, however, the Apostle deliberately invokes the brotherly fellowship which unites them. This form of address must help to restore the brotherly unity which has been threatened. Thus the polemics of the apostolic fighter end with a warm, brotherly word of encouragement.

The letter ends with the answering cry used by the communities in the liturgy: Amen. The customary affirmative answer at the end of prayers and blessings of the church is placed by Paul at the end of his valedictory blessing. But it holds good for the whole letter, which is to be read aloud in the liturgy of the communities. And then the Christian communities will also utter their " Amen." They will follow the Apostle along the way of grace and faith, of freedom and love.